THIS STARTLING, INTIMATE ... questions about the beginn... beginnings of the age of spi... daughter, was real, even to herself – apart from her pain? Stephen Foster's book is a wonderfully easy interweaving of wit, irony and scholarship, which also makes you wonder what history itself really is.

Emeritus Professor Alan Atkinson, author of *Camden* and *The Europeans in Australia* (3 vols)

HAVING DISCOVERED AN INTRIGUING STORY, Stephen Foster researched it diligently and fashioned an ingenious way to tell it. His book has many layers – biography, social history, Guernsey culture, art theory, historiography.... He brings the past alive, entertains and educates, and leaves the reader thinking. Literary groups will have enormous fun discussing this elegant volume.

Dr Gregory Stevens Cox, author of *St Peter Port 1680-1830: the History of an International Entrepôt*

A GRIPPING TALE of love and intrigue with many unexpected twists and turns which play with the sympathies and emotions of the reader. The story is told through contemporaneous reports and statements, and vividly through the imagined diary of one of the main participants. Added realism comes from the setting in old St Peter Port, which has changed little in the ensuing years. As an account of family discord and court battles, the story is painfully familiar.

Sir Richard Collas, Bailiff of Guernsey

WHAT A GOOD READ THIS IS! The result of extensive research into a bitter child custody battle in Guernsey in 1825, this book mixes classical scholarly historical narration (with endnotes), invented diary entries and details, and thoughtful reflections on the nature of history, truth, and fiction. An excellent example of historical fiction, or more accurately, I think, fictionalised history, it is bound to prompt many lively conversations – between friends, in reading groups, and in history classrooms. I was engrossed from beginning to end.

Professor Emerita Ann Curthoys, co-author of *Is History Fiction?* and *How to Write History that People Want to Read*

Zoffany's daughter

Love and treachery on a small island

Stephen Foster

SOUTH SOLITARY PRESS

CANBERRA 2017

Published by South Solitary Press, Canberra 2017

National Library of Australia Cataloguing-in-Publication entry
Creator: Foster, S. G. (Stephen Glynn), 1948-, author.
Title: Zoffany's daughter: love and treachery on a small island / Stephen Foster.
ISBN: 9780646971414 (paperback)
Subjects: Zoffany, Johan, 1733-1810
Horne, Cecilia, 1779-1830
Custody of children - History
Historiography - History
Guernsey (Channel Islands) - History
Designed by Adrian Young, Canberra
Printed by Excell Printing Group, Merimbula

Also published in the United Kingdom by Blue Ormer Publishing,
Cookham, 2017

www.zoffanysdaughter.com

Cover: 'one of the most beautiful women in England'. Zoffany's daughter
Cecilia cradles her son John in a conversation piece painted by Zoffany,
probably in 1803. Although this is long before the events recounted in this
book, it is Cecilia's only known portrait, and captures something of her
youthful beauty. John, the second of her eight children, died in infancy.
The painting is reproduced in full on page 33.
PRIVATE COLLECTION

Back cover: detail from 'View from Clifton, Guernsey', 1829.
The lithograph is reproduced in full on page 108.
PRIAULX LIBRARY, ST PETER PORT

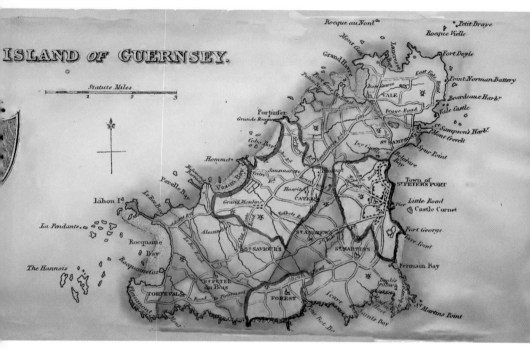

An Historical and Descriptive Guide to the Channel Islands of Guernsey, Jersey, &c. &c, J.E. Collins [St Peter Port], 1834.

CONTENTS

Most of this story is true.

So far as I know, none of it is false.

Much of it is fiction.

⮞ 'Nothing else is spoken of' ⮜

In October 1825 a report appeared in the London *Morning Chronicle*, headed

Matrimonial separation

GUERNSEY, *Oct. 4. – You can easily conceive what a sensation, in a small place like this, the arrest and committal to prison of an English lady, the wife of a clergyman, and evidently of rank and fashion, must create. Nothing else is spoken of. I transmit to you the few imperfect particulars I can collect of a story involved in doubt and mystery. The lady is the wife of the Rev. Mr. Horne of Chiswick …, and daughter to the celebrated Zoffany, the painter. It appears that she and her husband, after living together for many years, and rearing a fine family, separated in 1822, in consequence of some unhappy misunderstanding. The lady was allowed to take her daughters, and a maintenance of £300 assigned her. Mrs. Horne lived since that time in France, and latterly in the neighbouring island of Jersey, with her children, one of whom is a very fine and accomplished young lady of 18, and the other, about whom the mother is now involved, a girl of ten years of age. The Rev. Mr. Horne having heard that his wife was guilty of some irregularity of conduct (the truth or falsehood of which I have no means of ascertaining), determined to have his children from*

*her care, and applied to her to give them up;
but Mrs. Horne, who, it seems, has ever been
exemplary in her conduct as a mother, if not
as a wife, and much attached to her children,
refused to surrender either of them. …
The case has puzzled all the wisdom of the
Court Royale, which is not yet decided in
which way its fury is to be directed against this
strange and dauntless woman.*

This is how readers were introduced to the marital problems of
Cecilia and the Reverend Thomas Horne. Such stories at the time
were not unusual – after all, the malodorous relationship between
the Prince of Wales and his late wife Princess Caroline, had been
public property for decades.

But several aspects of this case made it remarkable: first, it involved a clergyman, part of whose job was to uphold the marriage
institution rather than help subvert it; second, his wife, as well as
being the daughter of a famous father, was well known in fashionable circles, and was reputed to have been a great beauty; third, the
contretemps involved the custody of a child; and most astonishing, the wife had the audacity to challenge what everyone at the
time assumed or knew – that a child was the property of its father.
And contrary to everything that might be expected of a woman,
especially an English lady 'of rank and fashion', she was prepared
to fight to keep her child even to the point of going to prison.
Whatever readers at the time might think of the rights or wrongs
of her challenge, they could scarcely avoid the conclusion that no
good would come of it.

I too first encountered the story of Cecilia and Thomas Horne
through a newspaper – to be precise, a clipping identical to the
Morning Chronicle report, but cut out from an Edinburgh broad-
sheet. It was located in a large family archive, in a file of other
clippings, letters and papers, none of which bore any apparent
relationship to it. The report seemed irrelevant to the research I
was then pursuing – yet I paused, intrigued by a narrative that
appeared at once remote and familiar. Indeed, stories about child
custody disputes today seem all too familiar, so much so that most

readers of this book probably know of one or more custody battles among their own circle of family and friends; at the least, they will know of cases that, for one reason or another, have entered the public domain, sometimes becoming *causes célèbres.*

The anonymous writer in the *Morning Chronicle* described a story shrouded in doubt and mystery. Perhaps the location added to the mystery. The small island of Guernsey in 1825, while owing allegiance to the British sovereign, enjoyed a distinctive culture, heritage and legal system; and most of its natives spoke their own dialect, based on Norman French. Cecilia Horne arrived there as a stranger, bringing with her legal and moral issues that most islanders had never confronted, and stood her ground in ways that few could have imagined. Little wonder she became the talk of the town.

This book is an attempt to unravel and tell the story – of Cecilia, the 'strange and dauntless woman'; of her elder daughter, Clementina, witness to almost all that eventuated, and my chosen storyteller; and of little Laura, the object of her parents' contention, whom we first meet dressed as a boy. It also tells something of those who judged Cecilia and those who tried to help her, or pretended to try to help her – for, as another newspaper remarked, the story is associated with 'a little treachery'.

It is also a story about history and how it is told.

⇒ Introductions ⇐

L ET ME INTRODUCE you to the Zoffanies.
      But first we should know how to pronounce their name.
W.S. Gilbert's very model of a modern Major-General provides
helpful guidance, rhyming 'The Frogs of Aristophanes' with
'Gerard Dows and Zoffanies', which suggests a short 'a'. Zoffany
himself, the great painter, probably pronounced it differently. He
was born, in 1733, near Frankfurt, Johannes Zauffalij, which was
transformed in Italy to Zoffani, then Anglicised after he arrived
in England in his late twenties. Whichever way he spelt and pronounced himself, he retained a strong German accent until his
death, in 1810, in London.

He has been called 'the Jane Austen of English painting'. If you
have never heard of him, there is nevertheless a fair chance you
have admired one or more of his paintings. He was prolific, pro-
ducing works inspired by mythological and historical themes,
portraits, conversation pieces, scenes from plays, and the occasional landscape. His canvasses hang in galleries and stately homes
throughout Britain and in many other parts of the world, from
Koblenz to Melbourne, Kolkata to Connecticut. He travelled restlessly, from Germany to Italy, back to Germany, then to England,
back to Germany and Italy, England again, on to India, then Italy
and Austria before returning to England. But for the prospect of
inadequate accommodation, he would have accompanied James
Cook on the great navigator's second voyage to the South Seas. He
later painted 'The Death of Captain James Cook', perhaps in small
compensation for missing an adventure.

He was buried at Kew, across the river from his home in Chiswick, and several paces from the tomb of Gainsborough. After
death he never achieved Gainsborough's fame, being generally
relegated to the second rank of English painters. Yet he was quite
a success in his lifetime, rising from modest beginnings as the son
of a cabinet-maker and architect in the court of a German prince,

acquiring plaudits and honours from Empress Maria Theresa, struggling at first in London, then rising through the patronage of the actor David Garrick, and winning favour in the Hanoverian court of George III and Queen Charlotte. He made at least two fortunes, struggled, according to a contemporary, with 'a kind of incontinence of the purse', yet managed nevertheless to leave his wife and children a respectable legacy.

Zoffany painted to please himself and make a living, which meant that he conformed to established artistic genres. He was no radical: the revolutionary upheaval in France appalled him. Some of his paintings, though, hint at rebellion, and (more than a hint) a readiness to cock a snook at pretence and hypocrisy; and certainly his family life set tongues wagging.

Around the age of 27 he married in Germany the daughter of a court official, who accompanied him soon afterwards to London. How long the marriage survived is not clear; but within a decade or so, his wife had returned to Germany and was never to see him again. In the meantime, Zoffany, who 'in his leisure-hours prowled for victims of self-gratification', had fallen desperately in love with (and/or seduced) a Jewish girl, Mary Thomas, aged about sixteen and the daughter of a London glove-maker. Armed with a commission to paint the Uffizi Gallery in Florence, Zoffany promptly decamped for Italy, perhaps with his lover's connivance or perhaps to escape an unequal relationship: whatever the case, Mary Thomas, who 'already bore the mark of criminality', appears to have smuggled herself aboard his vessel departing for France. The two lovers made their way together to Florence, where Mary gave birth to their first child.

Whether they actually married in Italy is uncertain. At one stage rumours circulated that he had been hanged for bigamy. What is sure is that both he and the first Mrs Zoffany lived on and far apart, and that Zoffany acknowledged Mary Thomas as his second wife. Their first child died tragically, following an accident; but the two went on to have four daughters and what appears to have been a relatively happy domestic life (perhaps nurtured by long periods of separation). In 1805 Zoffany's first wife died in Germany, allowing him to remove lingering doubts about his second. They were promptly, if quietly, married in accordance with Church of England rites at their parish church in London, recording their names

A family at tea: Zoffany, 'John, Fourteenth Lord Willoughby de Broke, and his family', oil on canvas, c1766. The artist captures an intimate family moment as the small boy on the left is pulled into line.
J. PAUL GETTY MUSEUM, LOS ANGELES

as 'Johan Zoffany … Widower' and 'Mary Thomas … Spinster'.

The four daughters, born unhurriedly between 1777 and 1796, were called Maria Theresa, after Zoffany's sometime patron; Cecilia, Claudina and Laura. Only the second, Cecilia, features in this book, though the others appear fleetingly. Cecilia Clementina Eliza Zoffany was born in Kew on 15 November 1779, soon after her parents had returned from Italy. A few years later, her father sailed for India where, in the customary way, he took a *bibi* and fathered a son. When he returned to England (without the son) in 1789, Cecilia was approaching her tenth birthday. Her father therefore missed five years of her childhood. She was, nevertheless, in manner and attitude, both her father's and her mother's daughter.

We owe what we know of her mother's character to her close friend, Charlotte Papendiek, of whom more later. She described Mary Zoffany glowingly, 'the friend of my youthful days … a perfect beauty, good-natured, kind, and very charitable'. It was 'always a holiday to go to see her'. When Zoffany first met her, wrote Mrs Papendiek, she had no education, but she remedied this during their seven years in Italy, learning to read and write English, and to speak

Italian fluently. She also acquired 'the polish of manner so essential to the position of a lady', so that 'her beauty, good dressing, and a natural elegance of appearance, combined with the feeling of happiness that shone in her countenance, soon fitted her for any society'.

Her early adventure as a stowaway in pursuit of her lover suggests that she was also brave and tenacious – though how much this early act of impetuosity, or desperation, tells of her later character must remain an open question. But whatever we might conclude about Mary Zoffany, there is no doubt that her daughter Cecilia was a woman of courage and resolution.

Johan Zoffany's personality emerges partly from the essence of his biography – the restlessness implicit in his travels, his hedonism and extravagance; partly from contemporary comments, including those of Mrs Papendiek – his underlying gentleness, masked at times by a mischievous wit, and his occasional outbursts of temper; but mostly from his art.

Take, for example, his group portrait from about 1766 of 'John, Fourteenth Lord Willoughby de Broke, and his family', which depicts the parents and their three children as they gather for tea. While the parents' pride in their children is manifest, the family is behaving as families do, with one son reaching for the bread or toast before he had been invited to do so, and the father admonishing him. Here is a naturalness and unsentimentality characteristic of the artist, and often missing from family portraits at the time.

Two decades later in India Zoffany captured a scene of exuberant decadence in 'Colonel Mordaunt's Cock Match', which depicts a match between Asuf ad-Daula, the Nawab Wazir of Oudh, and the English commander of his bodyguard, Colonel Mordaunt. This has been aptly described by an art curator as 'probably the most remarkable image engendered by the British involvement in India', raising 'significant questions about power relations, race and culture at a critical historical moment'. It is full of sexual innuendo, wry commentary and sardonic wit, some of it well concealed. In the centre of the painting, the Nawab leans imploringly, suggestively, to his right, towards one of his favourites. Although the Nawab kept a vast harem, he was well known at the time to be impotent. So Zoffany the humourist, presumably for his own amusement and for those who saw the painting before completion, gave him beneath his flowing kurta an impressive erection,

'Colonel Mordaunt's Cock Match', oil on canvas, c1784-6. Zoffany's painting says much about British life in India, and much about his own lively wit.

TATE GALLERY, LONDON

lately exposed by modern techniques of conservation.

Zoffany appears in 'Colonel Mordaunt's Cock Match', seated on the right at the rear, and seemingly bored with the proceedings. He painted himself often, never attempting adornment. Tall and balding, with a long straight nose, pursed lips and pock-marked cheeks, he seems to modern eyes an unprepossessing figure. Yet in late eighteenth century London he was an imposing presence, at the court, the Royal Academy, the theatre, and musical events on the Thames. So too his daughter Cecilia attracted notice wherever she went. Confident, intelligent, sharp-witted and articulate, she was a formidable woman.

She also had the advantage of being 'beautiful in the extreme'. We have that on the authority of Mrs Papendiek.

⇒ On gossip ⇐

CHARLOTTE PAPENDIEK has much to answer for. Born in London in 1765, she grew up within the milieu of the court of George III, her father serving as the King's principal barber and her husband as a court musician, doubling as barber when the King, descending into madness, became too fractious and excitable for her nervous father to shave. She herself became Assistant Keeper of the Wardrobe in the late 1790s and later Reader to Her Majesty the Queen, evidently retaining these appointments until the Queen's death in 1818.

Presumably in these situations she gave satisfaction, as did her father and husband in theirs. The reason she is remembered though (invariably as *Mrs* Papendiek) is a memoir she wrote long after the period she described. Here she presented a lively and intimate account of court events, people and fashions, and especially painting and music, over a period of some thirty years. Much of it is based on hearsay, much on personal observation – and much of it is wrong. She was, wrote Zoffany's (joint) first biographers in 1920, 'a garrulous old lady, who wrote about events long after they had transpired, and often mixed up dates and names in almost inextricable confusion'. But we should not be too censorious: the memoir was written modestly, for family consumption; if often wrong in detail, it seems faithful to the times; and it hints, however unreliably, at things we otherwise might not know, including information about the life and character of Cecilia Zoffany.

The raw data of Cecilia's life emerge from parish registers. She was born at Kew in 1779, the second daughter of Johan Zoffany and his 'wife' Mary; she married in 1799 the Reverend Thomas Horne, her elder by seven years, who taught in his father's boarding academy at nearby Chiswick; and she gave birth to eight children, all but one of whom survived infancy. London papers reveal that in 1821 her marriage became unravelled (leading to the events described in this book).

Mrs Papendiek, who was a warm friend of Mary Zoffany, embellishes this spare biography with observations about Cecilia's early childhood and marriage. She tells us that Cecilia and her elder sister, Theresa, when they were aged about eight and eleven, 'appeared to be amiable, but, poor dears, they preferred joining in all the domestic arrangements, and cared little for accomplishments'. We next meet Cecilia when she is about sixteen or seventeen years old, resisting the advances of a Colonel Martin, lately returned from India, with a castle in Kent and a vast fortune. 'She, foolish girl, refused this eligible offer and he retired to his castle disappointed and mortified.'

Cecilia, so Mrs Papendiek tells us, then 'contrived to fall in love' with the Reverend Thomas Horne of Chiswick, 'fearing that her father would marry her to some one she could not bear, as she termed it'. Horne, she says, was 'an amiable man, but extremely plain and not very prepossessing', who devoted himself to his father's school at Chiswick 'with universal honour and credit to himself'. Both families entirely disapproved of the match, but the two lovers were united, with both fathers attending the wedding and Zoffany recommending a reconciliation on all sides. Zoffany bestowed on the groom a dowry of £300, and placed £2000 in trust at three per cent for his daughter's benefit (a precedent he followed for each of his other daughters). Cecilia and Thomas, wrote Mrs Papendiek, 'had a fine family, and went on remarkably well.'

'Eventually, however, one circumstance and another brought on most unfortunate disputes, and the Horn[e] family interfering too severely and very injudiciously, Cecilia left her husband, and they were never again reconciled.' Likewise Cecilia's two younger sisters, now themselves married, were 'injudicious intruders' in the Horne household. Both sides had violent tempers, and when the two collided, the disputes between husband and wife, which ended so unhappily, began.

Then, without drawing breath, Mrs Papendiek hints at another possible cause of matrimonial unhappiness:

> It was never supposed by Cecilia's friends that she acted criminally. Indiscreetly, certainly; for as her beauty never faded with her increasing years, her vanity kept pace with them; but her unhappiness arose more from her dreadfully

passionate temper than from any other cause. She evinced resentment and vindictiveness to her husband and her children, who gave him great trouble.

So Cecilia emerges from Mrs Papendiek's memoirs as beautiful, vain, determined, wrong-headed, perhaps flirtatious (but not adulterous), and towards her husband, ill-tempered, resentful and vindictive.

What, though, is the worth of these opinions? Mrs Papendiek is wrong, for example, regarding Cecilia's first lover, the rich colonel, who was not in fact, as she implies, the painter's famous friend from his time in India, Colonel Claude Martin, but another, unconnected Colonel Martin. If we must doubt her facts, should we not also regard her opinions with the same degree of scepticism? Zoffany's descendants told his first biographers that, while Mrs Papendiek had been much attached to Mrs Zoffany, she did not like her daughters, and that accordingly 'many of the bitter things she mentions of the daughters were inserted in her diary in pique and are for the most part untrue.' But is this merely pique responding to pique?

Because historians and biographers have had little else to go by, Mrs Papendiek's views have been repeated from one book to the next (including this one!), usually with appropriate reservations; yet, through the very act of repetition, her gossip has been elevated to a status it probably does not deserve, and with it our expectations of Cecilia Zoffany and how in certain circumstances she might have behaved.

Let us return then to what we do know. Towards the end of 1821, Cecilia and her husband, the Reverend Thomas Horne, by now Rector of a lucrative London parish, separated, by mutual agreement, 'in consequence [as reports in the London newspapers put it] of some unhappy misunderstanding'. The unhappy parties, assisted in some way by Cecilia's mother, Mary, signed a separation agreement, which provided that Thomas should provide Cecilia with £300 per annum, payable in two instalments each year, for the next three years, suggesting that the parties viewed the separation as irrevocable. While the formal agreement made no stipulation about the children, Thomas evidently allowed Cecilia to take with her two of her three daughters, the eldest, Clementina, aged 13, and the youngest, Laura, aged just 6. The eldest son had attained his majority and was therefore free to do as he wished. The remaining daughter and four sons remained with their father.

Presumably the separation caused something of a scandal at the time, as any marital discord was likely to do, especially if it involved a clergyman and respected schoolmaster. Yet it seems to have escaped mention in the London press. During the next couple of years, the Reverend Mr Horne continued to teach at the Manor House School in Chiswick, and when his father died in 1824 he assumed the office of head master. Cecilia's movements are hard to trace. She seems to have decamped with the girls to France, and then (but who knows exactly when?) to Jersey, the largest of the Channel Islands. Here she was obliged to take in washing, suggesting that she was no longer

Women washing near Princes Tower. Jersey

While in Jersey, Cecilia was obliged to take in washing. 'Women washing near Princes Tower, Jersey', lithograph by G. Barnard; and Day & Hague; and published by M. Moss, Guernsey, 1841.

PRIAULX LIBRARY, ST PETER PORT

receiving maintenance from her estranged husband. This in turn suggests that she was determined to distance herself from him, even at the cost of a regular income.

In mid-1825 she and her daughters embarked on a short voyage from the port of St Helier in Jersey to St Peter Port, the only substantial town on the neighbouring island of Guernsey. Within several weeks, everyone on the island who could read newspapers, in English or French, or listen to people gossiping, knew of their plight. And almost everyone had an opinion about them, one way or another.

Let us imagine that they arrived on a specific date, 2 July 1825, shortly before Clementina's seventeenth birthday. Her mother, Cecilia, is now aged 45, and her sister Laura 10. Now, with my help, Clementina tells the story. I promise to make her every bit as reliable as Mrs Papendiek.

The journal of Clementina Horne

Madame Lihou's house
Smith-street
St Peter Port, Guernsey

Monday, 4ᵗʰ July 1825

Today being my birthday, my dearest Mama has presented me
with this handsome journal. I know it is a sacrifice for her, as it
was given her by a kindly gentleman in France, and I am sure
she had intended it for her own use. She tells me though that I
should get greater benefit from it than she. I am to keep a record
of our daily lives, and this she says will serve as a substitute for
writing letters to my relations and old friends. Dearest Mama is
anxious lest our frequent movements should have ill effects on
our education, but in truth I believe that she, through her dili-
gent instruction, has been able to confer benefit far greater than
any schoolmistress we might have engaged during our travels.

I am therefore determined to do justice to her generosity, to
keep a full and honest record of our lives, and to express myself
with all the care that I would apply to letters I might, in hap-
pier circumstances, have written to my brothers and sisters and
aunts and cousins in England. I am fearful that our lives are so
unremarkable and we are so far divorced from society that I
will have little to say. But Mama assures me that the subject of
my writing is of no consequence, so long as I practise my gram-
mar and penmanship, and that as she will not expect to read the
diary, I have only to satisfy my own conscience and the interest
of an imaginary reader.

We arrived on this island two days ago, after an uncomfortable passage from the neighbouring isle of Jersey. At one time
Mama had conceived that we might settle there, and had made
arrangements for Laura to attend a school run by a scholarly
lady who had once taught at Mrs Norton's at Blackfriars – and I
was hopeful of gaining employment with one of the bailiwick's
most respectable families. But it was not to be. Although dearest Mama had contrived to meet all our needs from within our
modest income, St Heliers, the main town, turned out to be more

expensive than she had anticipated, and before long we faced an accumulation of debts that seemed insurmountable.

I regard myself now as a seasoned sailor, even aboard the *Peggy*, the little packet that brought us hither. While Mama shares my strong constitution, this last crossing proved too much for her, and both she and Laura spent much of the short voyage sitting beneath a shelter in the centre of the boat, availing themselves of basins supplied by an attentive steward. This had the fortunate effect of removing the need for communion with the other passengers, some of whom were suffering equal distress.

Travellers on the pier at St Peter Port prepare to board their packets for England, Jersey or France. When Cecilia, Clementina and Laura landed, the seas were high and their landing was perilous. 'A view of Guernsey Pier and part of the town', lithograph by J. Taudevin and C. Haghe; and published by M. Moss, Guernsey, 1829.
PRIAULX LIBRARY, ST PETER PORT

When at last we sailed into the little harbour of St Peter Port, soon after dusk, a small flotilla of four-oared gigs was on hand to convey passengers and cargo to the pier. The sea was still high, and we were all quite drenched. As poor Mama lifted her skirts to step onto the landing, our boat suddenly lurched, causing her to slip – and were it not for the timely assistance of a vigilant deckhand, I believe she might have fallen between the boat and the stone landing, with consequences too appalling to contemplate. Poor Mama appears to have twisted her ankle, which means that she has so far been unable to leave our lodgings. Fortunately she seems to have sustained no lasting damage, and is chiefly concerned lest the drama at the landing place draw unwanted attention to our arrival.

With the help of our landlady in Jersey, a proficient seamstress, Mama has fabricated a splendid blue and white sailor's costume, which allows Laura to assume the disguise of a boy. During our time at St Heliers she played this role convincingly, though not without protest, as Mama also insisted that her hair should be cropped short. This has rarely been achieved without tears, as Laura is, or rather was, inordinately proud of her golden locks which once extended beyond the line of her waist. Mama tells her that her disguise is essential to our concealment, and I tease her by saying that cabin-boy clothes are in the latest fashion, and that she would be the envy of the young sons of dukes and earls. But I fear she remains unpersuaded.

We were fortunate when we landed at St Peter Port to be met by a young man, Monsieur Peter Lihou, who loaded our trunks onto a small cart and helped us along the causeway and up the hill to his mother's house in Smith-street. We have been able to secure two small rooms, one with a bed sufficient to accommodate myself and Laura, and the other of about the same size, where M. Lihou, who is a carpenter by trade, has installed a sofa bed for Mama to sleep on. This place will serve well enough for a short while, but Mama hopes we can find somewhere more commodious and less exposed to public view.

Mme Lihou is a widow-lady, whose husband died many years ago in the Peninsular War. She is by profession a hairdresser and perfumer, and her house is in fact a shop in a long row of shops in one of the busiest parts of town. She is plump and a little bumptious, and very business-like, but I think well-meaning. Her first words to Mama were to tell her that two weeks' lodgings would be payable in advance – then, when Mama had assured her that she was able to pay, she pressed us to remove our damp clothes instantly lest we catch cold, and asked if we should be needing a fire – which of course was unnecessary, as the weather is exceedingly warm. Although she appears to take in washing, she speaks and acts as if she were our equal. From our few possessions and shabby dress, she would have no reason to think otherwise.

Yesterday, after attending church, she accompanied me in a quest for alternative lodgings in the island's interior. We had not walked far along the Catel road when we encountered an elegantly attired gentleman, who greeted Mme Lihou by name in a most unaffected way, then removed his hat and bowed politely to me. Mme Lihou, assuming her most ladylike demeanour, introduced me, saying that I had recently arrived on the island with my mother and younger brother, and that we were in search of more permanent accommodation. The gentleman responded that he would be happy to show us a house that was soon to become available at Le Villocq, near the centre of the island, and that he hoped he might have the pleasure of calling on Mama and myself the following morning. His name is Mr Jean de Jersey, and Mme Lihou tells me he is a member of one of the island's most genteel families. I have great hopes that he will prove a true friend.

Tuesday, 5th July 1825

True to his word, Mr de Jersey called this morning to pay his compliments to Mama. In anticipation of his coming, Mama and I were seated in Mme Lihou's parlour behind the shop, with Laura remaining concealed upstairs in our bedroom. As soon as Mme Lihou ushered him in, I could tell that his impression on Mama was immediate and favourable, for his appearance and manners are extremely prepossessing. He is tall, but not excessively so, about the same age as Mama, and yet with a full head of dark hair, a neat beard, and penetrating blue eyes, which command the attention of the person with whom he is conversing. He has an open countenance and a most engaging smile, which immediately puts one at one's ease, and a deep mellifluous voice.

As with many people we met on Jersey, he speaks with a gentle accent which must be French in origin, yet differs pleasingly from the more effusive enunciation of native Frenchmen when they endeavour to speak in English.

As his manners and deportment would suggest, Mr de Jersey is a gentleman of ancient family and immense wealth. He also told us that his brother is His Majesty's Comptroller on this island, which is a very high legal office, and his father, who had passed away, had long served as a Jurat, which is like a magistrate – his uncle is the Lieutenant-Bailiff – and he is proprietor of an extensive property at Le Foulon in the island's interior. He promises to call on us again tomorrow morning, when Mama and I will accompany him to see the house that is available for rental.

This evening Mme Lihou served supper early. While there was still sufficient light, Mama allowed Laura to accompany me on an exploratory tour of St Peter Port, enjoining us to remain inconspicuous and, should need arise, maintain our deception as Miss and Master Miller, the aliases we had assumed in Jersey. We descended our street until we came to High-st, which is in fact the lowest street in the town. This is lined on both sides by an unbroken row of shops and houses, some of them four storeys high, some with bow windows, and most of them unremarkable. Indeed, were it not for frequent signs in French at the shop fronts, the overall appearance resembles an English country town. Some streets are so narrow that residents might lean out from their third storey windows and shake hands with neighbours across the road. Another peculiarity is the drain that runs down the middle of paved streets, similar to those we had noticed in French towns. Laura nearly slipped into one of these at the bottom of Smith-st, causing a soldier who was coming down the hill towards us to call out Careful Laddie! which caused her to grip my hand tightly and her face to redden in embarrassment.

Mme Lihou gave us strict instructions on how to avoid be-coming lost, which would indeed be easy to do, for as soon as we left High-st we entered a maze of steep and narrow roads, steps and laneways lined by shops and houses that seemed indistinguishable from one another. We passed close by several old ladies in their quaint bonnets and full dresses, chattering at the corner of one lane, but fortunately they seemed too engrossed in their conversation to notice us. After passing through the covered market place, we climbed a long stone staircase which our landlady tells me has lately been constructed for the benefit of ladies and invalids. I found the climb – almost 150 steps in all – invigorating; but Laura complained much of the way and had to pause frequently to recover her breath. Her long confinement has left her wanting in energy.

'View of the town of St. Pierre-Port, from the Lower Newground. Guernsey', drawn by G.S. Shepherd; lithograph by L. Hague; and published by M. Moss, Guernsey, 1829. The grand, castellated building on the right is Elizabeth College; the tower of St James's Church dominates in the centre; and the Town Church is at the far left. PRIAULX LIBRARY, ST PETER PORT

At the top of the hill the bunched-up houses suddenly give way to hedged paddocks, interspersed by thickets of luxuriant vegetation. We discovered a fine vantage point which afforded a splendid view of the port, which is dominated by an ancient fortification known as Castle Cornet and which occupies the whole of a rocky outcrop not half a mile from the shore. The little harbour was crowded with sails, as well as the new steam packet that plies between here and Southampton. In the far distance, beyond the islands of Herm and Sark, we could see a few flickering lights, which must be the coast of France.

We then wound our way along the top of the hill, as far as possible keeping the sea within sight so as not to lose our way. Once on the plateau we glimpsed several magnificent two- and three-storey mansions, separated by plantations of orange and pear trees, and each surrounded by fine gardens with an abundance of flowers, including a profusion of Guernsey lilies, yet to bloom, and the most splendid hydrangeas I have ever seen.

I wonder if one of the mansions belongs to our new friend Mr de Jersey. Several hundred yards on we reached a park called the New Ground, with seats and well-constructed paths for promenading. Several couples, including a man in officer's uniform and his lady holding a splendid blue parasol, were taking the evening air, but we skirted around the perimeter and I think managed to remain unnoticed. From here we descended a rough unpaved lane towards an ancient castellated ruin called Ivy Castle, which Mme Lihou had told us to watch for, and shortly came upon the long esplanade that straddles the shoreline. This was damaged by a violent storm last winter and much of it is still in need of repair. It is lined on one side by a muddy beach which I understand can disappear entirely when the tide is high, and on the other by a row of shops, warehouses and houses as high as five storeys. Now we re-entered the maze and made our way back to our lodging house. We had traversed the most settled parts of the town in a little over an hour, without losing our way.

On our return to the shop we encountered a young person whom I had taken to be Mme Lihou's servant. She is a plain and sallow-faced girl, somewhat older than I am, and evidently resentful of our presence. She made no effort to introduce herself – and had not Mme Lihou entered the shop as we commenced our way upstairs, we would have had no idea that she was in fact our landlady's daughter. Mama says that she probably speaks no English and assumed that I understood no French – but I suspect she is merely sullen and unpleasant. Her name is Elisabeth, and she lives with her mother on the top floor of the house. I will do my best to avoid her. There is one other resident, a Mme Berryman, who is Peter Lihou's mother-in-law. Mme Lihou told me that she lives at the back of the house on the ground floor, but I have not yet set eyes on her.

Thursday, 7th July 1825

Yesterday, soon after we had taken breakfast, Mr de Jersey rang the bell beside the door of the shop and invited Mama and me to accompany him to see the house at the Villocq, on the Catel road, some two miles from our current location. Almost everyone walks in St Peter Port, owing to the steepness of the roads; but when we reached the top of the hill, Mr de Jersey, no doubt remembering Mama's painful ankle, had a gig waiting to take us the rest of the way. The house is a modest stone dwelling, and appears to be in good repair, with an excellent well of good water, a small apple orchard, and a vegetable garden, now somewhat overgrown, but with the potential to meet our own needs as well as supplement our income. Mama believes this might serve our purposes very well, but worries that the cost of rental will exceed our means. Mr de Jersey tells us that in recent times many genteel families, including officers returned from the wars and now on half-pay, have come to settle on the island, where the prices of food and furnishings are generally lower than in London. These *rentiers* have added to the island's prosperity, which has been languishing since the end of the wars; but they have also forced up the cost of lodgings.

On the way home Mr de Jersey spoke about his own ventures and aspirations for this island. As one of the bailiwick's foremost agriculturalists, he implements the latest modes of cultivation and has introduced several improvements on his estates. He told us of his efforts to improve the situation of his tenants, which Mama warmly commended. He is also engaged in numerous commercial enterprises, including importing timbers from

Sweden and Norway and exporting apples and potatoes to England. Although he was eager to show us his seat at Foulon, he was unable to do so as his builders are currently undertaking repairs to the staircase. We did however pass the house of his brother the Comptroller, on the Grange road, which is indeed a splendid edifice.

Mr de J then asked Mama – without in the least exceeding the proper bounds of inquiry – about how she and her family came to be on the island. Mama told him that her son (meaning Laura) had a constitution of the greatest delicacy, which was much improved when not exposed to cold winds – and that accordingly we had resided for some time in France and Jersey before coming hither. Then, with a degree of agitation, she hinted at our difficult financial circumstances. He was clearly moved by our situation, and asked if he might lend us his assistance, to which Mama replied that both she and I intended to seek employment and that we could live peacefully on a cow's grass, so long as we were free from pecuniary distress. Then, without hesitation, Mr de J took his purse from his handbag and removed three pounds, which he thrust into Mama's hand. She of course protested, but he insisted that she accept the money as a loan that she might repay when we are properly settled on the island.

This is an enormous relief – and while dearest Mama is troubled by being beholden to Mr de J, I doubt that she could wish for a kinder and more solicitous benefactor.

Saturday, 16th July 1825

I confess that my resolution to make daily entries in this journal was too ambitious. So little has happened to warrant recording. I am determined, though, to try harder, and to recount our lives on this island at least once a week.

Mme Lihou remains friendly and solicitous and her daughter surly and ill-natured. We have now met Mme Berryman, M. Peter Lihou's mother-in-law, a pale and thin old lady without a tooth in her head. We chanced upon her as she was heading out to the Town Church, where she sweeps the floors twice a day. She greeted Mama and me civilly enough, but as we climbed the stairs to our room we heard her whispering to Mme Lihou – and while I could not catch what she was saying, I doubt that it was in our favour.

Dearest Mama's ankle is now much improved, and she now descends the stairs without difficulty. Yesterday evening before supper we stepped out for the first time as a family, Mama and I wearing our best walking dresses and Laura in her cabin-boy costume. We walked along High-street as far as the Town Church, then in the opposite direction along Pollet-street and the esplanade known as Glategny, pausing on our return to watch a packet lately arrived, we suspect from France or one of the other islands. A group of men who appeared to be supervising the unloading looked quizzically in our direction and then began nattering among themselves, and an old gentleman and lady addressed us directly with 'bonjour', the gentleman removing his hat; but otherwise we were little noticed.

Laura asked how long she would be obliged to dress as a sailor boy, and Mama replied not much longer, though I doubt that this can be so, as people will wonder how a boy can suddenly become a girl. Laura said nothing in response. I know she is yearning to cast the disguise aside – but she also understands that she must wait until Mama is certain it is safe to do so.

Saturday, 23rd July 1825

The population of St Peter Port being small, we encounter the same people whenever we step out of our lodgings. I cannot say this town is especially hospitable towards strangers. While some whom we pass in the street say 'bonjour', they sometimes accompany their greeting with a knowing look – though it is surely impossible that they should know anything of our real circumstances. They speak to one another in an odd sort of French, and to us in broken English – except of course Mr de Jersey, whose English is eloquent and refined. He has visited us several times and towards Mama he is particularly solicitous – I believe he regards her with genuine admiration. He has promised to show us his mansion at Foulon, just as soon as the carpenters have finished the latest improvements. Lately he has taken receipt of a large consignment of superior building timber from Sweden, and has been busy arranging its distribution throughout the island from the timber yard on

Glategny. I asked M. Peter Lihou if he was engaged in Mr de J's renovations, but he was not aware of them.

This past week Laura has been ill again, with a violent fit of nervous asthma. On Tuesday her fever was so high and she was suffering such shortness of breath that Mama asked Mr de Jersey if he knew of a medical gentleman who could be trusted not to speak of our circumstances. He recommended Dr O'Brien, who lives close by at the top of our street. He came immediately and said that the fever was due to the recent insalubrity of the air. After bleeding Laura, he gave her an expectorant, which put Mama at ease. Laura was much improved by the evening – though whether this was due to the doctor's ministrations, or the fever running its course, I cannot say. The doctor seemed to look oddly at Laura, and I feared that he had discovered her secret – but if he did in fact have suspicions, he kept them to himself.

A notice has appeared in the *Star* offering tuition in the French language. The teacher, M. Bott, claims to have a method of conjugating verbs which transforms conjugation from an arduous task to an entertainment, and ensures that pupils will acquire a rough knowledge of all the forms of any verb within a few hours. As my French is barely adequate, such lessons would undoubtedly improve my prospects of securing a situation with a good family in one of the rural parishes, where French is mostly spoken. But the cost is £3 a quarter, which is well beyond our current means.

Sunday, 7th August 1825

Today Robert will be 15 years of age. I have not seen him or my other brothers or my sister Cecilia since we quit London over three years ago. I miss them all beyond measure, and wish I could at least write to them. But I dare not ask Mama again, as any communication would multiply her anxieties.

This morning we attended church, for the first time since we set foot on this island. Mama decided that we should attend the Town Church, where French is spoken, rather than St James's, where services are conducted in English for the officers and soldiers of the Garrison. The Dean in the Town Church, M. Durand, gave a sermon on the Lord's Commandment to love thy neighbours; after which, as we left the church, a young lady about my age introduced herself to me and asked if she might be my friend. I was a little taken aback by her presumption, but nevertheless agreed that we should meet before church next week. Her name is Mlle Major, and she is the daughter of a proprietor of one of the island's French newspapers. I think I shall like her very well.

Mr de Jersey remains attentive, visiting us every morning and sometimes taking tea. Today he waited on us in the evening in Mme Lihou's drawing room, Laura having withdrawn in anticipation of his arrival. Mama offered him a small glass of Madeira, which he accepted, and took one herself. Then he gently enquired why, having spent time in the warm climes of France, we had chosen to come to this island and whether she intended that we should stay. Much to my surprise, Mama told him of our predicament, admitting that our names were not Mrs and Miss and Master Miller, and that Laura was not in fact a boy. And then she said: my husband treated us cruelly in London and we were obliged to part in regrettable circumstances.

Mr de J was clearly astonished, saying that while he hoped Mama would not consider his interest impertinent, he had indeed suspected that our appearances belied our station in life, and that he feared we had fallen on hard times.

Mama then explained that her father and our grandfather was the late illustrious painter, Mr Zoffany, at which information Mr de J expressed further amazement, declaring that while he had not been privileged to view any of the great artist's works, he knew that he was renowned as one of the finest England had known. And that while he was deeply saddened to learn of Mama's matrimonial troubles, their brief friendship was sufficient to convince him that she was a lady of the highest principles, and that she could not have parted from her husband except under the gravest duress.

Until this point in the interview, Mama had retained her usual composure; but now her face reddened and her lip trembled, and I feared that she was close to tears. Even in arguments with Papa and Laura I had never seen her so distressed, and I had to avert my own eyes. Mr de J looked in my direction and was clearly embarrassed, having realised that his questions had exceeded proper decorum. I think at that point he would have made an excuse to take his leave, had not Mama immediately proceeded to speak more of the events that had led us to leave England. During this account she implied that Papa had unfairly questioned her, and otherwise treated her ill. I do not like to hear Mama speaking of Papa in such terms, and therefore begged leave to be excused, declaring that I had suddenly remembered a chore I had promised to perform for Mme Lihou.

I then strolled down the hill and along High-street, as far as the Town Church. By the time of my return, Mr de J had departed, and Mama had entirely regained her customary serenity.

I should have mentioned that Mme Lihou has offered to rearrange the first floor so that we might have to ourselves a small drawing room, with a view over the street. This will be a great addition to our comfort.

Wednesday, 10th August 1825

Yesterday evening Mr de Jersey invited us to accompany him on a walk into St Andrew's Parish, where he had some small business to discuss with one of the agricultural proprietors. The distance was under two miles in each direction, so Laura, her health being much improved, had no difficulty keeping up. Our route out of town took us up Mont Durand, where many new houses are being built, then up a steep hill to a crossroads, which presented a splendid vantage point for viewing the southern parts of this island. Here, just short of his intended destination, Mr de Jersey paused, and pointing to a cross rudely carved on a large stone at the side of the road, told the following story.

Five or six hundred years ago, after these islands had ceased to be part of France, there was a despotic Bailiff who owned a grand estate close to this spot. One of his poor neighbours owned a patch of land at the back of his house, which gave him an ancient right to draw water from the Bailiff's well. This annoyed the Bailiff so much that he endeavoured to acquire the peasant's land. When this failed, he determined to rid himself of his irritant forever. Concealing two silver cups in a rick of corn, he created evidence which proved that the peasant had stolen them. Then he had him charged with theft and larceny, the penalty for which was death.

The trial took place and the unfortunate peasant was condemned to die. But on that very morning, the Bailiff had ordered his men to move one of his ricks into his barn. The men mistook his command and moved the wrong rick, in which they discovered the missing cups. One of them ran to the courthouse, where he announced to the Bailiff and magistrates – the cups are found! The cups are found! The Bailiff, caught unawares, responded instantly – you fool, you moved the wrong rick! The magistrates apprehended the Bailiff's wickedness and, without further ado, sentenced him to death. On the way to the place of execution, his gaolers allowed him to pause at this very spot so that he might take the Holy Sacrament – and ever after this place has been known as the Bailiff's Cross.

At this point in the story Mr de Jersey ran his finger along the cross on the granite stone. Mama expressed relief that evil should be so justly rewarded, and made as if to continue our walk. But Laura, who had been listening intently, grasped Mama's skirts, and begged that we should go no further and return immediately to town.

But the story is not yet over, said Mr de Jersey, and he proceeded with greater animation: When the peasant, assuming he was free from persecution, next went to the well, he was confronted by the ghostly form of the Bailiff, his arms pinioned, and his face in the agonies of death. Beside him was the appalling vision of Satan in the guise of a dragon, with barbed tongue and frightful fangs, and breathing fire and brimstone. The peasant ran away, terrified – and thenceforth, whenever he went to draw water, he was attended by this ghastly apparition. Eventually he decided to sell his plot of land and moved far away, where he was free from persecution. But the Bailiff's ghost remained to haunt the well and all the land around it, including where we were then standing.

Mr de Jersey paused for a few moments, and then said: even today, when unexplained shadows and apparitions appear anywhere on the island, Guernsey men and women know that they have been visited by the Bailiff's ghost.

When he had completed his story, Mr de Jersey eased away from us and sat down on a rock, lowering his head as if deep in thought. I did not know what to make of the story, which seemed to lack any moral, or Mr de J's telling of it, which he did with more spirit and energy than I thought it deserved. Was he merely trying to amuse us, or was he warning us of unexpected dangers? Mama seemed much agitated, though later she made light of it. Laura said nothing, and shortly we realised she was shaking with fear. Mama and I tried to pacify her, telling her that it was only a story, but she remained petrified, breathing rapidly, her brow damp with perspiration. Fearing that this might presage another attack of the asthma, Mama slapped her, which brought her partly to her senses, and begged Mr de Jersey that we terminate our excursion and return to town, which he instantly acceded to. We took the shortest route possible, by way of the Grange, and by the time we reached home, Laura's colour had returned and her pulse was no longer racing. Mr de Jersey was clearly alarmed by Laura's reaction to his story, which no doubt he has told many times before. He probably thinks of her as a feeble boy, even though he knows otherwise.

Friday, 12th August 1825

Mama has sent me to M. Greenslade's, the grocer in High-street, to purchase a ticket in the lottery, which is to be drawn at the end of the month. Papa had always been violently opposed to lotteries – but Mr de J told Mama that, as parliament had resolved to end them, this was the last chance to win a large fortune from a very small sum of money. There are four grand prizes, each of £25,000.

Walking along the Pollet, I chanced upon Mlle Mauger, the young lady who introduced herself to me at the Town Church. Her father is proprietor of the *Gazette de Guernesey*, one of the town's three French newspapers. She speaks good English, softly, with a slight accent and a pronounced lisp, which conveys an impression of vulnerability, though I suspect she is as capable and confident as any of the young ladies of her rank and education. The young ladies of Guernsey are reputed to be great beauties, and she must surely be estimated high amongst their number. She was on her way to Mme Agnew's to see the latest bonnets from London. While the superior classes on this island may *sound* French, they look to London for the latest fashions.

Mr de J visited as usual this evening. When Mama expressed

anxiety about the increased cost of our lodgings, he said that she should give no thought to it and that so long as we remained on his island he considered it his duty to ensure that we would want for nothing. He lent Mama £2 for clothing, saying that her beauty should be shown to best advantage. I thought this was remarkably forward of him, but Mama did not take it amiss.

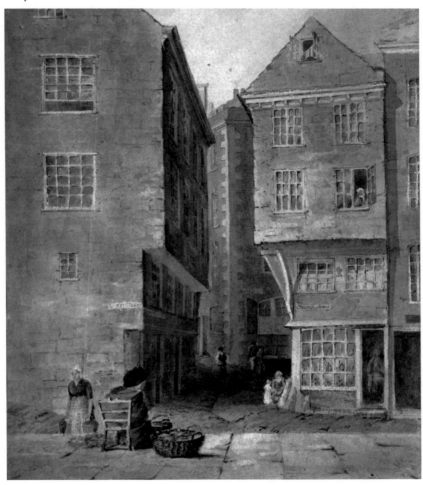

'Looking up Fountain Street, 1825', watercolour by Peter Le Lievre (1812-1878), probably painted some decades later but depicting 'Old Guernsey' from the artist's memory. The street rises from near the waterfront, with shops on either side. In the foreground a hawker, perhaps from Brittany, displays her wares.

GUERNSEY MUSEUMS & GALLERIES, ST PETER PORT

❧ On history & pictures ❧

As Zoffany was renowned as a portraitist, and Cecilia acclaimed as a beauty, surely we can hope that he painted her. And so he did. But we must tread warily, for paintings can often deceive.

Zoffany appears to have been especially prone to misinterpretation, in part perhaps because the artist left so little record of his own life other than his paintings. His foremost exponent, Mary Webster, curator of an exhibition of his works in 1977 and author of a magisterial study in 2011, remarked that his biography and works have been subject to 'fiction and falsification', culminating in the first published biography in 1920, which she described as 'a dangerous book'!

Yet Webster herself has not escaped a savaging, or at least suggestions that she lacked imagination. Take for example the sharply conflicting interpretations of a self-portrait painted by Zoffany in Italy in 1779. The painting is two-sided, in more ways than one. On one side of the panel is a saintly depiction of the Holy family during their flight into Egypt. On the other is what seems at first glance to be another religious painting, in which the artist portrays himself donning a friar's robes. Behind him on the wall hangs a string of rosary beads, flanked on one side by a small print of Titian's voluptuous *Venus of Urbino*, her lower regions chastely obscured, and on the other by two cat-gut condoms. On a shelf above them are playing cards and a carafe of wine, further symbols of a hedonistic life.

The experts differ about what the self-portrait means. Does the donning of a monk's attire imply, as the visual language of the era suggests it might, that the artist is renouncing worldly pleasures, perhaps at a time of personal and spiritual torment? Or is he putting on a familiar disguise in preparation for a night on the town? Mary Webster affirms the former. Recent scholarship supports the latter, explaining that Zoffany is mocking his then patron, Duke

Ferdinando of Parma, who notoriously combined religious devotion with debauchery. Happily, we don't need to take sides (though the discovery that Venus's modesty is protected not by a tear in the canvas but by a third condom strongly supports the case for a night on the town). Either way, the painting serves as a reminder that, while historians should use whatever visual sources are available, they must – as they do with written records – handle them with care.

The art of concealment 1: Zoffany, 'Self-portrait with Friar's Habit', oil on panel, 1779.
GALLERIA NAZIONALE DI PARMA

The art of concealment 2: Zoffany, 'Mary Thomas, the Artist's second Wife', oil on canvas, c1781-2.
ASHMOLEAN MUSEUM, UNIVERSITY OF OXFORD

Zoffany painted several works depicting members of his family – perhaps many, though only a few are known to have survived. There is a portrait of his 'wife' Mary, seemingly gentle and sweet-natured, dating from the early 1780s, before his long sojourn in India; and a conversation piece, from about the same time, showing his eldest daughter, Maria Theresa. Theresa, as she was usually known, is the subject of a later canvas which is now lost or missing, though the likeness is preserved in a photograph.

'Zoffany and his children', oil on canvas, c1803. Compare Cecilia, far right (and on the cover), with the portrait of her mother, Mary Thomas, at much the same age.
PRIVATE COLLECTION

Sadly, there is no known portrait of Cecilia. There is, however, an unfinished conversation piece alternatively titled 'Zoffany and his children', 'Zoffany with his Daughters and Two Grandsons' and 'Portrait of the artist with his Family', which depicts the artist painting his family as some of them play various musical instruments. So far, so good – but who exactly appears in the painting is open to debate. The 'dangerous book' from 1920, which drew on family memories, did not name all the daughters, but identified the woman holding a baby as an old family nurse. Later scholars agree that this could not be right, as the supposed nurse was 'much too young and fashionably dressed'. But confusion remains. Penelope Treadwell, author of a 2009 biography of the artist, dates the painting from 1799 and has Cecilia at the harpsichord (or spinet), while her mother, the baby's grandmother, holds the child. Mary Webster, who dates the work from 1802-3, has the eldest daughter Theresa playing the harpsichord, while Cecilia is cradling her second-born child, John. Apart from the artist himself, every figure identified by one scholar is identified differently by the other!

In this instance, Webster's interpretation seems persuasive. The names she assigns to the sitters correspond with their apparent ages; Theresa, not yet married but soon to be so, is not wearing a married woman's cap or hat; and Cecilia, appropriately hatted, is married with two young children. Furthermore, Theresa closely resembles the two other likenesses that bear her name. Cecilia has no other portrait for us to compare her to. She does, however, closely resemble her mother's earlier portrait – the deep eyelids, the straight line of the nose, the high cheekbones, the finely shaped chin, the overall proportions – the most obvious difference being that Mary is looking up and Cecilia is looking down. Cecilia, at about the same age as her mother, looks sadder, perhaps more reflective – as well she might have been.

This, the only known likeness of Cecilia, depicts her more than twenty years before she arrived in Guernsey. Now, in 1825, English newspapers remarked that she had once been 'one of the most beautiful women in England, and though pretty well in years, at the matronly side of forty, she still possesses strong marks of her former loveliness, and adds to them the attractions of an accomplished woman and dignified carriage.'

Beyond these clues, visual and verbal, Cecilia's appearance, like much else in this story, must be left to our imaginations.

The journal of Clementina Horne

Madame Lihou's house
Smith-street
St Peter Port, Guernsey

Monday, 15ᵗʰ August 1825

We are discovered! Mama is thrown into confusion and Laura cannot be consoled.

On Saturday last I set out early towards the butchers' bazaar, intending to purchase a partridge from one of the women who bring their produce from Brittany. As I entered the High-street I halted suddenly, as there before me were my father and my brother Thomas, accompanied by Papa's friend, the chemistry professor Mr Brande. Fortunately I remained unnoticed, as they disappeared promptly within Mme Tozer's boarding house, where I concluded they were staying. I instantly abandoned my shopping expedition and hurried back to Mme Lihou's.

Our pursuers had evidently arrived from Southampton that morning aboard the steamboat *Ariadne*. I cannot doubt that Papa intends to persuade dearest Mama to return to Chiswick and resume her duties as wife and mother. Who could have alerted them to our presence on these islands? Is no place on earth secure?

Since then I have noticed two constables, whom I recognise from having seen them at the markets, idling a short distance up the hill; and I think they followed me when I stepped out later with Mme Lihou. I have not told Mama about them, lest it cause her even greater anxiety.

Yesterday we avoided church – but to what avail? Mama said she could not bear to meet Papa in a public place and needed time to collect her thoughts about what to do next, hoping perhaps that we might escape this island unnoticed, or find refuge in the interior. Her misery is indescribable, for she had come to believe that together we might make a new home on this island.

We have since remained closeted in our upstairs quarters and have seen no-one, apart from Mme Lihou and her unlovely daughter. Our landlady must wonder at our secrecy, but she is a kind-hearted soul and does not presume to enquire. Mr de Jersey visited on Saturday morning at his customary time, but Mama instructed Mme Lihou to say that she was not in a position to receive him. He came again yesterday after dinner, expressing concern that we were not at church that morning, and Mama again put him off. But the presence of three strange gentlemen in town must soon be noticed, so that he and everyone on the island must soon know of our melancholy situation.

Tuesday, 16th August 1825

From the lines beneath her eyes, I perceive that Mama has not slept at all last night. When I rose from bed, she told me she is determined to confront Papa directly. From first light this morning the three of us have taken turns sitting by the window, with the curtain adjusted slightly to allow an uninterrupted view down the road as far as High-street. This would at least allow Mama a few moments to steel herself as Papa climbed the hill.

But Papa did not appear. A little before nine o'clock, a gig struggled up the road and deposited outside the shop Thomas and Mr Brande, who alighted and knocked on the door. In keeping with Mama's directions, Mme Lihou showed them in and seated them in her parlour, and then came upstairs to announce their arrival. Mama and I descended to meet them, telling Laura – who was eager to see her big brother – to stay out of sight. Mama and I embraced Thomas, who seemed unwilling to meet our eyes, and then she acknowledged Mr Brande, who bowed very low. Mama, having sensed her advantage, began the interview in a strong voice, saying: My dear son, I am indeed surprised to see you on this island. Have you come to fetch us? And then, immediately, she asked about his brothers and little Cecilia, all of whom, thanks be to God, are well, but he said, full of sorrow that they had for so long been separated from their mother and sisters.

Mama then turned to Mr Brande and addressed him thus: Sir, might I ask what brings *you* here? Are you engaged in chemical experiments? (which I thought was remarkably cool of Mama, in view of our predicament).

Mr Brande replied to the effect that the circumstances of his being there are more appropriate to a private interview, hinting that I should withdraw – but Mama said: I am sure there is nothing you can impart that would alarm Clementina or that I would wish to keep from her – and as you evidently intend that my son should remain present, then so should she.

He then said: my dear Madam, I must tell you that we have accompanied your husband to this island (here Mama and I feigned surprise) and that at this very moment he is lodged at an inn not far from here, awaiting our return. His purpose, Madam (and here he paused to wipe the moisture from his balding pate), is to urge you to resume the position in society that society expects of you. The reverend gentleman (he said) had exhibited as much Christian charity as might be expected of any man; indeed, he believed it was impossible for a man to show more of the proper affection and duty of a husband. But the period stated in the deed of separation, which he had so unadvisedly entered into and so honourably adhered to, had now expired: and it was now time for Mrs Horne to return to London and resume her place as duteous wife and helpmeet to her husband and attentive mother to *all* (he said pointedly) her children.

And so he went on in this vein, with many vehement ahems and much talk of duty and obedience, which Thomas endeavoured to endorse by appearing earnest and solicitous, while trying to avoid meeting our eyes.

Mama, having planned her tactics in advance, allowed Mr Brande to run his course, forbearing to respond even when he gave the impression that he would have welcomed an interruption in order to gather his thoughts. Then, when he had obviously done, she said:

I thank you, Mr Brande, for your concern on behalf of my family, and for the troubles you have taken in coming so far. Please convey to Mr Horne my assurance that nothing will induce me or my daughters to return to London, or indeed to leave this island, where we have established a comfortable home.

Mr Brande then declared that, while he was reluctant to speak of such things, his friend was dismayed to hear reports that his daughters were not receiving an education and upbringing consistent with their position in society; and that while Mr Horne had yielded to their mother's entreaties when the original deed was written, and had allowed two of his children to accompany their mother, the time had now come that they should take their places by his side and enjoy the benefits of which they had latterly been so regrettably deprived.

As Mama remained silent, he then rose and bowed, saying that he would convey her response directly to Papa; and Thomas, who had hitherto said almost nothing, looked directly at Mama with a pained expression and said: dear Mama, I do hope you will give earnest consideration to what Mr Brande has had to say, for if you don't, it is unpleasant to contemplate what might ensue – and with that, followed Mr Brande out the door.

Shortly after they had departed, Mr de Jersey, who must have been aware of their visit, arrived to pay his compliments. Mama was scarcely able to disguise her agitation. She explained that Papa had lately arrived on the island, and she rehearsed the interview that had just taken place with his emissary. I fear, she said, that my husband will stop at nothing to ensure that we accompany him to London and may try to remove my dear girls by force – this, she said, is an intolerable prospect – I would rather pass the rest of my days isolated from human contact than spend another night beneath his roof. I can manage without the £300 a year he is supposed to pay me – and I would willingly hand over the £2000 I have in London if only my beloved daughters might remain with me.

Mr de J was obviously deeply moved by Mama's distress, and told her to set her mind at ease – she had on this island staunch and influential friends; and should Papa attempt to remove her against her will, he would find Jean de Jersey at her side.

Thursday, 18th August 1825

No sooner had I recorded the foregoing than we heard yet another knock on the door below, followed by Mme Lihou's trundling along the corridor and calling Mama to come promptly, as a constable had a message for her. Mama descended and returned shortly shaking with anxiety, and with a piece of paper in her hand. Papa insists that Laura and I come home with him – and as Mama has said she will forbid this, he has applied to the Royal Court on this island to enforce his demands. Accordingly, we are required to appear before the Court tomorrow at noon.

Until now, Mama had borne all these vexations with her usual fortitude. But when Laura asked: Mama, does that mean I will no longer have to wear this hateful sailor costume? she burst into tears.

Saturday, 20th August 1825

Mr de Jersey, having discovered that we had been summonsed, proposed that he accompany us to the Royal Court, which offer Mama gratefully accepted. And on his suggestion, Dr O'Brien, who had attended Laura several times during her recent afflictions, joined us outside the Court. I had walked past the Court House before: it is a stern, two-storey stone building in Manor-street, half-way up the hill, high above the road behind an iron railing and a broad empty pavement. Mr de Jersey, who seemed familiar with every part of the building and all its occupants, led

'... it is a stern, two-storey stone building in Manor-street, half-way up the hill, high above the road behind an iron railing and a broad empty pavement'. 'Royal Court. Guernsey', drawn by de Garis; lithograph by C. Haghe; and published by M. Moss, Guernsey, 1829.
PRIAULX LIBRARY, ST PETER PORT

us to a spacious and imposing room on the upper storey, with a high ceiling and sufficient benches, raking to the rear of the room, for perhaps a hundred onlookers – though when we arrived there were just a few men scurrying around in black gowns, and an old woman busily polishing the elevated semi-circular bench which is the main feature of the room. On the walls are grand portraits of men whom I assume to be local dignitaries, busts of our King and his father George III, and in a niche a statue of 'Justice' with her blindfold and scales.

One of the men in black ushered us to seats in the front row of benches on the left of the aisle, and Dr O'Brien sat down on the bench behind us. Mr de Jersey chatted affably with another of the men in black before sitting beside Dr O'Brien, immediately behind me, while several men entered through the rear door and seated themselves on the vacant benches. A short while later, Papa entered as we had done, by the side door, accompanied by Thomas and Mr Brande, and two men whom I took to be his attorneys, and proceeded to the seats immediately to our right. Mama stiffened as she caught sight of Papa, and looked at him directly, and I forced myself to follow her example; but Papa, who looks much older than when I last saw him, pretended to be in close conversation with Mr Brande and one of his lawyers, and did not even glance our way. Thomas, who had brought with him two large law books, fingered through one of them until, on looking up, he discovered something in the scales of 'Justice' that demanded his undivided attention.

Then two men wearing black gowns and birettas strolled in purposefully, and took their places in the lower pew benches on the left and right of the main bench. They were followed by a tall, dignified officer of the court whom we had noticed as we entered the Court House. He stood at his own table in the centre, immediately in front of the bench; and as the clock behind us struck twelve, he called in French for everyone to stand. The chief magistrate now entered from a side door, followed by seven other magistrates, all resplendent in gowns and high birettas. Mr de Jersey leaned forward and whispered that the chief was the Bailiff, and the others were called 'Jurats'. Once they were seated, with Bailiff in the centre, the tall man, whom Mr de J called 'the Greffier', rose again and proceeded to speak at great speed in

French, which I was not prepared for. Fortunately Mama has an adequate grasp of the language, and mine was sufficient to catch his meaning. Papa, on the other hand, mastered Greek and Latin, but was never called upon to teach French at the Manor House, so in this respect at least we were not at a disadvantage.

It is easier to write of the appearance of the Court Room than of what then transpired, which was brief and distressing. The tall man proclaimed that the court had convened to hear the Reverend Thomas Horne's claim that his daughters should be returned to him. The Bailiff then, in perfect English, asked Papa to state his case. Papa then rose and read from a prepared speech, to the effect that, nearly four years since, Mama had *unnaturally* abandoned her husband and family; that he had allowed myself and Laura to remain with her and had provided for them generously, not realising that she intended to live abroad. For a long time, he had been unaware of their whereabouts. But lately, having discovered where and how they were living, he had endeavoured to persuade his wife to return the children to him, which she had obdurately refused to do. He therefore had no choice but to appeal to this court to uphold his rights as a father over his minor children and demand that their mother return them forthwith.

Papa began his speech hesitantly, as I remember him doing when he delivered a sermon, becoming louder and more emphatic as he continued. But just as he was warming to his subject and appeared to be embarking on a lengthy exposition, he evidently thought better of it, and resumed his seat.

The Bailiff then asked Mama if she had anything to say. She stood very upright, in her usual way, and turned directly towards Papa, whose eyes were still fixed on the Bailiff, and then said: nothing can exceed the love I feel for my daughters, and no court can break the bonds of affection between us. And then, to the Bailiff and the Jurats: I would rather die than be separated from them – at which point Laura began to sob, and Mama became distracted and unable to continue.

As she was embracing Laura and trying to console her, one of the two men who had entered separately and who was seated at the bench to the left of the Jurats, began an oration, entirely oblivious of Mama's distress. Mr de Jersey leaned over and said to me: this is my brother, the Comptroller – and I could see then a family resemblance. He too is of striking appearance, but with a more severe countenance than his brother, whom I assume to be some years younger, and no beard. I fear that, unlike Mr de Jersey, we will be unable to count him as a friend.

The Comptroller, whom everybody referred to as *M. Contrôle du Roi*, spoke in French – but his enunciation was precise and the gist of his argument was clear: 'the father has an incontestable right to the possession of his minor children'. And as he pronounced those words '*un droit incontestable*' he raised his right hand, as if to forestall any argument. Laura, who was gasping for breath between her sobs, then cried out: please do not make me return to Father, I cannot bear to think of such a thing, and began to wheeze alarmingly. Mama turned to the Bailiff and said: Sir, you can see the prospect of separation is too much for my daughter to bear, at which the Bailiff looked at me and said, Mademoiselle, do you too wish to remain with your Mama – to which I of course replied that I did. And Dr O'Brien, who had stepped forward to assist Mama and Laura, then begged to be heard, telling the Jurats that if mother and child were to be so suddenly separated, he feared for the health of both.

The Bailiff then summoned to the large bench *le Contrôle du Roi* and the man who had entered with him and engaged them in several minutes' conversation, all of which of course was in French. *Le Contrôle du Roi*, who spoke with much animation, finally threw up his hands, as if in disgust; and the other man, whom the Bailiff called *M. le Procureur*, summoned Papa and his entourage to join them. There followed prolonged discussion in both French and English, though as their voices were lowered I was unable to catch many words. Everyone then resumed their former places, the Bailiff consulted among the Jurats, and then called the court to order.

Then he repeated those dreaded words: '*le Père a un droit incontestable à la possession de ses enfants mineurs*', at which Mama drew breath audibly. But he went on: observing the distressed state of the mother and younger daughter, and hearing the evidence of M. le docteur about the dangers that would ensue from a forced and sudden separation, the Court has decided that the mother might keep the two daughters until the 1st September – less than a fortnight from now.

Mercifully, Papa yielded that I might remain with her as long as I wish, adding kindly that I will always be welcome in his home. This concession – entirely unexpected – has done much to ease my mind, as it will allow me to do everything in my power to ameliorate poor Mama's anxieties. I fear though it will be small compensation for Laura being wrenched away from us.

Having delivered the Court's judgment, the Bailiff ordered that constables be stationed outside our house to ensure that Laura did not escape. He then said, in a compassionate voice, that this would not be necessary if Mama swore an oath that she would safely deliver Laura on the appointed day. I thought Mama would immediately accede to this proposal, but she responded:

'Gentlemen, I thank you for the confidence you are willing to place in my word of honour. I will instantly prove to you I deserve your good opinion. I will not forfeit my integrity by taking such an oath, even though by doing so I might secure to myself the child I value more than my life! Ask your own hearts – look back to history – and tell me, did you ever hear or read of a woman who deserved that name that would not, for her Lover! – Husband! – or what is far more dear, her Child – brave all dangers? Place therefore what guard you please: for as I live, were it in my power, I would win my way with her through ten thousand guards!!'

We walked back to our lodgings in desolation, escorted by Mr de Jersey and Dr O'Brien. Two constables followed us, several paces behind.

⇒ On the history ⇐ of child custody

SIR WILLIAM BLACKSTONE, in his famous *Commentaries on the Laws of England,* first published some sixty years before Cecilia Horne confronted the laws of Guernsey, explicated with his usual authority the law as it applied to parents and their children. Parents, he wrote, had three duties to their (legitimate) children: to provide for their proper maintenance; to protect them; and, by far the most important, to give them an education suitable to their station in life. These duties necessarily gave parents power over their children, for without such power parents would be unable to perform their duties. Blackstone drew attention to ancient Roman laws, which, he observed, gave fathers the power of life and death over their children; and while this power had later been softened, Roman fathers had continued to exercise 'very large and absolute authority'. In England, the power of a parent was 'much more moderate; but still sufficient to keep the child in order and obedience'.

There was scarcely need for Blackstone to comment at this point on the respective powers of fathers and mothers, for this had been adequately covered in his preceding chapter on husbands and wives. Here he explained the ancient principle that 'By marriage, the husband and wife are one person in law'. That is, except under specific circumstances, the woman had no separate legal existence. Her 'condition' during marriage was defined by the term 'coverture'; and while Blackstone conceded that marriage imposed on the wife some legal disabilities, these were for the most part intended for her protection and benefit: 'So great a favorite is the female sex of England.'

So when he passed to the subject of parents and their children, the power of the mother – or rather, her lack of power – was mentioned merely in parentheses, in the context of asserting that the legal power of a father ceased when a child reached the age of twenty-one '(for a mother, as such, is entitled to no power, but only to reverence and respect)'.

Blackstone did not claim the father's powers were absolute, as they supposedly were in ancient Rome; and in practice the Court of Chancery, which dealt in matters of equity, did take note of the interests of children, especially where there was some doubt that the father was able to provide for them. Nevertheless, in Blackstone's striking phrase, 'the empire of the father' still held sway. And if there were any movement in English courts and public opinion to question it, this was abruptly halted by the revolution in France, where the sacred institutions that held society together appeared to be falling apart. Even the family appeared to succumb to revolutionary zeal. New laws in the early 1790s defined marriage as an exclusively civil contract, admitted divorce on various grounds, and allowed mothers to have custody of all children under seven as well as older girls, with fathers having charge of older sons. In fact, these changes were not as great as anxious spectators sometimes assumed, for French customary law, applicable through much of the country, had long acknowledged the rights of mothers. In any case, a decade later the Napoleonic Civil Code went a long way to restoring paternal authority. But viewed from England, the assault on the traditional family seemed yet another instance of revolutionary excess, which, if allowed to cross the Channel, might undermine the foundations of English society.

So English courts held firm to the notion of paternal authority. A sensational case – or rather, two related cases – in the early nineteenth century was symptomatic of the times. In 1804 Margaret de Manneville, who claimed that her husband treated her cruelly, escaped from beneath his roof and went to live with her mother, taking her eight-month-old baby with her. The husband, Leonard Thomas de Manneville, a French national, came to the grandmother's house and removed the baby. Shortly afterwards, with the end of a short-lived peace with France, the father was incarcerated as an enemy alien and the child returned to its mother – only to have the father, once released from prison, revisit the grandmother's home where, in the words of contemporary reports, he snatched the child 'then at the breast, and carried it away almost naked in an open carriage in inclement weather'.

The mother, a woman of independent means, applied to the King's Bench, so becoming the first woman in England to sue her husband for custody of their child. The court, which dealt in matters of common law, declined to interfere, interrupting arguments in the mother's favour by declaring that the father 'is the person entitled by law to the custody of his child'. Undeterred, she turned to the Court of Chancery, which was notionally more liberal and humane than the King's Bench, urging that 'children of such a tender age ... cannot without great danger be separated from the mother'. Here too her pleas were rejected on the grounds that, as a married woman, she could not bring suit against her husband – in other words, while she was in a condition of coverture.

The decision in the de Manneville cases caused a public outcry, which was no doubt intensified by the husband being a Frenchman; but it brought no immediate changes to the law or the way the law was administered. During the next thirty-five years, mothers sued for custody of their children just seven times and succeeded only once, when the father was in prison under sentence of transportation, and therefore clearly unable to fulfil his duty of providing for the child. Even in cases where fathers were deemed to have behaved cruelly or immorally, the courts were reluctant to interfere with paternal rights that were so well established and so widely understood. Only when the mother had died, and the doctrine of coverture was therefore not an issue, were judges prepared to transfer custody from a father deemed especially odious to that of a relative or other guardian – as in the case of the poet Shelley, whose notorious lifestyle and libertine opinions were considered far beyond the pale.

Other cases around this time captured public attention, but none seriously challenged 'the empire of the father'. There was, for example, the harrowing contest between an Irish peer, George Nugent, Marquess of Westmeath, and his wife Emily, daughter of the Marquess of Salisbury, which began in the courts in 1819 and dragged on for some fifteen years, a case involving brutality, adultery, large sums of money, and the custody of their surviving child. In 1825, when Cecilia and Thomas Horne appeared before the Royal Court in Guernsey, it still had many years to run.

Not until 1839 was there a major change to the law of custody. This owed much to the determined lobbying of Caroline Norton – celebrated author, and friend and confidant of the Prime Minister, Lord Melbourne – whose husband had subjected her to physical abuse and kept her apart from her sons. Norton, drawing on the de Manneville case and other cases that had captured public attention, and joined by other determined women, including Lady Westmeath, overcame heated opposition and won support for legislation which allowed mothers to seek custody of their children up to the age of seven as well as access to older children. Their efforts culminated in the passage of the Infant Custody Act, which, while it had little immediate bearing on court decisions, was a clear statement that mothers did have rights. It also set a precedent for parliament to intervene in custody issues.

For those who longed for change, it was tortuously slow in coming. In 1873 parliament allowed the courts to give mothers custody and access to their children under the age of sixteen, as well as introducing the principle that courts could take into account the welfare of the child; and in 1886 courts were actually *required* to consider the welfare of the child, and the conduct and wishes of both parents. It was not until well into the twentieth century that legislation in Britain provided that the welfare of the child was to be 'the first and paramount consideration', and that neither mothers nor fathers had a superior claim to custody.

Cecilia and Thomas Horne appeared before the Royal Court in Guernsey some two decades after the de Manneville case and more than a decade before the passage of the Infant Custody Bill. Both Cecilia and Thomas might have remembered the de Manneville case, which was widely reported at the time. Both surely knew of the accusations and counter-accusations being hurled between Lord and Lady Westmeath. Likewise, the legal fraternity in Guernsey were probably aware of past and present custody cases in England; and if they were unfamiliar with specific cases, they would at least have known and understood contemporary English assumptions about paternal authority. Certainly, they were well acquainted with Blackstone.

So we can fairly assume that exchanges in the Royal Court owed something to past precepts and present debates in England on the custody of children. Whether the Horne case had any influence on later changes to the laws of England is another matter. Perhaps Caroline Norton and Emily, Lady Westmeath, as they lobbied politicians during the 1830s, remembered the short reports of events in Guernsey that appeared in the London newspapers, or some of the gossip about the vicar and his errant wife that surely circulated at the time. But the Channel Islands scarcely figured on the mental map of most Londoners; and Guernsey law, as we shall see, was far removed from English jurisprudence, so that while legal men in Guernsey might look to the various London courts for guidance or precedent, the chances of any London judge or attorney looking in the opposite direction were close to nil. In the legal history of child custody in England, the Hornes were never likely to rate a mention.

Yet there is more to the history of child custody than changes in public opinion and legislation. Another history records the thoughts, feelings and emotions of those involved in child custody battles, and the scars that often outlived them. That history, which moves beyond testimony in the law courts, has so far been told chiefly through the microhistories of individual families and the eyes and pens of novelists. Larger histories, in which the story of the Hornes should find a place, have yet to be written.

The journal of Clementina Horne

Mme Lihou's house

Tuesday, 30th August 1825

The last ten days have stretched almost beyond endurance.
Mama refuses to allow Laura to step beyond the threshold of
the house, for fear that she might be kidnapped. As there is no
piano here for her to practise on, she passes the time reading. Dr
O'Brien, who has two young daughters, has been kind in bringing her picture books and fairy tales and other books suitable for
her age. She has just finished *Stories of Old Daniel* and is about to
start *Oriental Tales*. The three of us play cards, and sometimes we
are joined by the mother-in-law, old Mme Berryman.

Laura has become more than ordinarily sulky, and takes issue
with everything I say. Once she begged Mama to let her accompany me into the town, but Mama persuaded her how foolish that
would be. As she has been outdoors only twice since we arrived on
this island, I suppose we must make concessions to her ill-humour.

Mama too has not left this house, except when she was obliged
to attend the Royal Court. On Mr de Jersey's suggestion, she had
Papa arrested for not paying the £300 which has been due to her
every year. I am sure Papa is in the wrong, as the pension should
have been paid several weeks ago – but I wish Mama had not had
him arrested. The scheme in any case failed, as there is a curious
law on this island that rules that a stranger cannot be imprisoned
for debt unless he has resided here for a twelvemonth. Thank-
fully, Papa was detained only a few hours. Mama then threatened
to appeal against the decision, but Papa sent his attorney to say
that he had no objection to paying the money once Laura is sur-
rendered on the 1st of September. Papa has now left the island,
accompanied by my brother and his disagreeable Freemason
friend, Mr Brande, leaving his attorney to collect Laura and take
her home to Chiswick.

As Papa has conceded that I might remain with Mama, I am
at liberty to leave the house at will, which allows me to take my
daily walk along Glategny. Several times I have met my friend

Mlle Mauger, who tells me that people in the town are exceedingly interested in Mama's circumstances and that there is much sympathy for her plight. I hate to think we are the subject of gossip, but it could scarcely be otherwise. Each time I leave the house I am reminded of our predicament by the presence of one or two of the constables, idling just across the road. Mr de Jersey makes light of them, and indeed they are a comical trio. Constable Tow, who is tall and bespectacled, performs his duties with ostentatious diligence, standing, pacing and peering in our direction as if adhering to a military routine. Constable Touzeau, who is portly and dishevelled, seems chiefly intent on nabbing the occasional passer-by for conversation. Constable Gallienne, who is mostly on watch in the night time and early morning, has much difficulty staying awake – I have seen him sometimes sitting on the steps of M. Robotham's boot shop across the road with his head resting on the door jamb and his mouth wide open, which must be exceedingly uncomfortable.

Mr de Jersey remains uniformly solicitous. On one of his morning visits, when Mama was briefly out of the drawing room, he took my hand and said: you and your dear Mama must put your anxieties aside, as I am confident every thing will turn out well. I cannot be so certain. Mama says we must trust in his judgment, for we have no-one else to turn to.

As Mr de Jersey's timber yard is not far from here, he insists that it is no inconvenience for him to visit us often. Lately we have seen him several times in the evening and he and Mama have consulted long into the night. I have missed some of these conversations, as I have been upstairs with Laura – but I have gleaned sufficient to know that he and Mama are trying to think of means of removing Laura from danger. M. Peter Lihou told me one day that he was engaged on important business for Mama, but what transpired I cannot say.

Wednesday, 31st August 1825

The dreaded moment has arrived. M. Mellish, one of the High Constables of St Peter-Port, came to tell Mama that he would collect Laura tomorrow and pay the £300 that Papa had promised, and to ask what time would suit.

'Part of the Town of St. Pierre-Port from Glatney. Guernsey', drawn by T. Compton; lithograph by L. Haghe; and published by M. Moss, Guernsey, 1829. Young street-sellers head out of town, while the gentry promenade along the sea-wall. Smith Street is located behind the closer of the two piers that enclose the harbour; the spire of the Town Church is visible in the middle distance.
PRIAULX LIBRARY, ST PETER PORT

While he was speaking, I tried to think how I might ease Mama's distress and comfort Laura. Yet Mama seemed unperturbed, calmly telling M. Mellish that she would surrender Laura at ten o'clock and that she would no longer exist after being separated from her child. M. Mellish said that he would hand over the money in bills of exchange, but Mama insisted that it be in cash in British currency.

I was astonished that Mama remained so collected, until after the constable had left she whispered to me that Mr de Jersey had spoken to her thus: 'if Laura could be got out of the house, he knew a particular friend of his, a french gentleman, who would take her in'. The name of the gentleman is M. de Campourcy, and Mr de Jersey describes him as 'a man of the strictest honour and respectability'. At Mr de Jersey's suggestion, Mama is now writing him a letter. Mr de Jersey is confident that our safety is assured.

A letter from Mme Cecilia Horne to M. Louis-Prudent De Campourcy

Wednesday, 31st August 1825

Sir, - *knowing the goodness of your heart, permit me to beseech you to protect*, for a few days, *the little child that presents you this.*
Ah, Sir! you had once a mother! By the recollection of her tender care in your infancy, I do pray you to judge of my agony in the bare idea that if you refuse my little petitioner, I lose her for ever!

The journal of Clementina Horne

The Prison, New-street, St Peter Port

Friday, 2nd September 1825

Surely Mama did not imagine it would come to this. Last night we spent in prison – or rather, in a room in the gaoler's house that is available for people with the means to pay – or, as in our case, others who will pay for them. There is no table in this room, but there are two beds and a chair, so that I can sit low on my bed with legs crossed and write on the chair. But I cannot write straight – and my mind is so troubled I find it hard to record how we arrived in this pitiable situation.

On Wednesday night, knowing that the constables were to come for Laura the next day, none of us were able to sleep. At 11 o'clock we heard a gunshot some distance away, which set the dogs barking, and Mama said – half-seriously I thought – that someone was probably coming to shoot her.

Mr de Jersey remained closeted with Mama until midnight. When he left, Mama came upstairs and explained to Laura what was about to happen, telling her to dress as usual as a sailor boy. Laura by now was in great distress and I tried to calm her, but I fear that her sobbing could be heard by others in the house, as Mme Lihou and Elisabeth came several times to see that all was well with us. Mama summoned me and my sister to kneel with her, and offered a brief prayer for our safety, after which we all recited The Lord's Prayer. Then we waited.

Soon after three o'clock Constable Gallienne arrived, as he usually does, to take over from Constable Tow. Mama immediately stepped outside and accosted them, complaining that the barking dogs had kept her awake most of the night and urging them to do something to silence them. The moment I heard them speaking, I reached for Laura's hand and together we crept down the stairs and along the corridor to the window facing the laneway, which had been left ajar, with the shutters open. I helped Laura to the ground, then led her along the high road to Mr de Jersey's town house in New Paris-road. At that hour there was not a soul to be seen on the streets. We walked silently, without exchanging a word. The sky was overcast, so I am sure no one noticed us. I left Laura, bravely trying to suppress her sobs, with Mr de Jersey, and the two promptly disappeared down the lane.

Confident now that I would not be seen, I ran home along Glategny. Shortly before daybreak Mr de Jersey came to the door and, taking care that Constable Gallienne was out of earshot, whispered to Mama that Laura was safely confined where no one would find her.

I then lay down fully clothed on our bed and drifted into a troubled sleep, only to be suddenly awakened by a loud knocking on the door. It was already ten o'clock, and Mama was wide awake – I doubt that she had closed her eyes during the night. She appeared to be well prepared for the call that we all so much dreaded. Mr de Jersey, who had returned in the early morning, opened the shop door and the three of us stepped into the street. There, as expected, was M. Mellish, accompanied by an assistant constable and M. Ozanne, who was one of the attorneys whom I had seen in the courthouse with Papa.

M. Mellish announced, superfluously, why they were there, and produced a large wad of bank notes, which Mama proceeded to count. Then she counted it again, gave it to Mr de Jersey to look after, and asked me to fetch a pen and ink to sign a receipt. M. Mellish then said: now Madam, where is the child? – to which Mama replied: *Take her if you can find her*. This threw the three men into confusion. The attorney said: come, come Madam, this will not do, and M. Mellish instructed the assistant constable to conduct a search of the house.

After several minutes, the constable emerged, followed by Mme Lihou and Mlle Elisabeth, and declared: indeed, sir, she is not here, she is nowhere to be found. M. Mellish, whose face had reddened alarmingly, turned to Mama and said: you must therefore return the money I have just given you. Mama responded: no sir, the money is justly mine, and addressing Mr de Jersey said, put it in your pocket and by no means surrender it. But before Mr de J had time to pocket the money, M. Mellish seized him by the collar and thrust him against the wall, while the second policeman lay his hands on his coat. Recognising that further resistance was in vain, Mr de J handed back the notes, and the three made off post-haste down the road.

An hour later M. Mellish returned with six or seven other men and demanded that Mama and Mr de Jersey and I accompany them – and so, as half the population of this miserable town gaped from their doors and windows, we were escorted up Smith-street and past the courthouse to our present place of confinement.

⇒ On small history ⇐

ALTHOUGH REPORTS ABOUT 'Mrs Horne and her child' reached the pages of no less a journal than the London *Times*, Cecilia's story is essentially a small one, involving a few members of a single family and those who came into contact with them, and narrowly circumscribed as to time and place.

The time, from the likely date of the family's arrival at Guernsey to their last mention in the local press, was nine months; the place, an island small in both area and population, albeit the second largest of the Channel Islands, after Jersey. Its furthest extremities are some fourteen kilometres apart, and its circumference – taking into account bays and inlets – about sixty kilometres, suggesting that Clementina, had she wished to do so, might have walked briskly around the whole island, without losing sight of the sea, and without being delayed by hedges, bogs or garrulous farmers, in a couple of days.

In 1825 Guernsey had a population of about 22,000, more than half of whom lived in St Peter Port. The town, which straddled part of the island's eastern shore, looking towards France, had expanded in recent decades beyond its medieval perimeter, so that there were now identifiable 'old' and 'new' towns. The former was characterised by ancient and run-down houses and shops in steep and twisted lanes, accommodating mostly the poorer classes; the latter, further up the hillside, by spacious and elegant terraces, with carefully tended gardens, some even with elaborate conservatories, and catering mainly for the middle classes. Beyond there, where the hill plateaued, localities such as the Grange and Hauteville presented still higher levels of prestige and salubrity, with classical villas, designed by English architects and set in expansive gardens.

A census conducted in 1827 showed that *natifs*, or those who were married to *natifs*, outnumbered *étrangers*, including those who intended to settle permanently or were just passing through, by a majority of more than two to one. The definition of '*natifs*' was very broad, encompassing those of ancient ancestry as well as relative newcomers who had made their home in the town. Many of the island's inhabitants proudly traced their ancestry back to medieval times and beyond. Indeed, according to one observer, Guernsey was 'the most pedigree-spot in the world', where a family who claimed ancestors in the tenth century scorned to associate with another who merely found links with the fourteenth. There was plenty of new money, including merchants who had enriched themselves during the recent wars and English soldiers on half-pay. But unless they could establish ancient origins on the island, 'an eternal barrier' was raised against them. And so it went throughout society, with 'divisions and sub-divisions extending to the butcher's daughters, bounded by impassable barriers, which neither wealth nor intermarriage can affect'.

In other respects, though, immigration had long helped fashion the island's culture. For centuries, the main influences had been French, and this had been reinforced in the late seventeenth and early eighteenth centuries by Huguenots escaping persecution on the Continent, and in the late eighteenth century by refugees fleeing the revolution in France. More recently, English immigrants had come to dominate, so that by the mid-1820s a third or more of the town population was English.

These changes were reflected in how people talked. Guernsey had its own *patois, guernésiais*, based on Norman French, which in the 1820s was still generally spoken in the rural parishes and widely used in the town. It was sufficiently distinctive that visitors from France, or indeed one of the other Channel Islands – which had their own dialects – might have had difficulty making sense of it. Standard Parisian French was no doubt spoken among recent arrivals from the Continent; and formal legal French remained the official language of local government and the Royal Court. But English was increasingly the language of the superior classes, with ancient landowners, wealthy merchants and fashionable young ladies about to enter the marriage market all keen to adopt English manners, dress and speech.

St Pierre-Port yielded to St Peter Port. English shops were opened alongside French ones, and French signs reappeared in English. 'La Grand Rue' became High Street, 'Rue du Marché' Market Street,

and 'La Rue des Forges', where blacksmiths once wielded their hammers or other smiths their tools of trade, and now Cecilia and her daughters took lodgings, became Smith Street. The people, or at least the town dwellers of Guernsey appear to have been remarkably well read, with a busy circulating library and, at the beginning of 1825, no fewer than four weekly newspapers, three in French and one in English. Just over a decade later there were three English papers, each published twice a week, and just one, a weekly, published in French. Not that French names and French influence were expunged suddenly or entirely: today street names still display their French equivalents, and a few old timers out of town still communicate with one another in *guernésiais*.

As a free port, St Peter Port had long thrived on trade, handsomely augmented from time to time by smuggling and privateering. Following the Peninsular War, the economy had languished. But now it was experiencing a revival, helped along by improvements in shipping. Several packets plied regularly between St Peter Port and Weymouth, Southampton, and other English ports, as well as the other Channel Islands, and St Malo and Cherbourg in France. And from 1824 steamers began servicing the island, with the *Ariadne*, 195 tons, departing Southampton for Jersey and Guernsey every Tuesday evening and, weather permitting, arriving in Guernsey the following morning. With them came the latest news from London, as well as a steady stream of visitors, who might seek accommodation in no fewer than seventeen hotels as well as numerous lodging houses. Mr Noel, proprietor of one of the hotels in the middle of High Street, saw which way the wind was blowing, and 'changed, at considerable expense, his *Café*

Detail from 'Plan of the Town of St. Peters Port and Environs', engraved by John Wood; printed by Turners & Co., Edinburgh, 1843. Smith Street, where Cecilia and her daughters lodged with Mme Lihou, is immediately inland from the North Pier of the enclosed harbour. A short distance to the west is St James's Church, marked in red, and opposite the church, the prison. New Paris Street is near the north-eastern corner of the plan, and Mont Durand Road leads out of town towards the south-west. John de Jersey's name appears on a large estate at the west and centre of the plan.
The distance, as the crow flies, between opposite diagonal points is about 2 kilometres.
PRIAULX LIBRARY, ST PETER PORT

Français into a French and English hotel, which may be termed splendid'.

Yet despite its increasing links with the outside world, Guernsey was figuratively as well as literally insular. While the people of St Peter Port might look to London for the latest fashions and furniture, and through their newspapers follow events in other parts of the world, they remained chiefly interested in themselves. Long term residents were a distinctive breed, and believed their distinctiveness was something to be cherished. Many families, especially among the ruling elite, were joined by marriage or friendship; others were connected through employment or trade; and those who were not in some way related might well have recognised one another by sight. Guernsey was, in other words, a small place, sheltered from the preoccupations of the rest of the world, and correspondingly absorbed in its own.

Here then, in the story of Cecilia, Clementina and Laura at St Peter Port, is a small series of events, interesting but seemingly inconsequential to all but those caught up in them, unfolding over a short time in a confined and inward-looking place. These, on the face of it, are potential ingredients of what historians call 'microhistory'.

Academic historians, like anthropologists, literary scholars, management consultants, and many other followers of a discipline or profession, are much influenced by fashion (though historians are perhaps slower to follow trends than most). Over the past half century, movements in the writing of history have come and gone, and sometimes come again – Marxist, empiricist, narrative, structural, labour, historicist, environmental, feminist, quantitative, social, nationalist, trans-national, total history, deep history, post-modern, cultural, new historicist, and many more. In recent decades it became fashionable to speak of historiographical 'turns' – hence the linguistic turn, the emotional turn, the digital turn, and so on. While some of these fashions were, for a time, *de rigueur*, none captured the whole discipline, and all contributed, in varying degrees, to how historians went about their business.

Microhistory has been one such fashion. The term has been used at least since the 1950s, when it appeared in the title of an intensive study of the final charge at Gettysburg, which lasted just twenty minutes. But microhistory as a recognisable genre is usually seen as having its beginnings among Italian historians in the 1970s, who were in part reacting against the aridity of traditional institutional and legal history in their own country, as well as to French historiography, highly fashionable at the time, with its emphasis on quantification and the *longue durée*. Sometimes it is seen as a postmodern reaction to the 'grand narrative' approach to historical explanation, though few microhistorians would describe themselves as postmodernists. Among the genre's most prominent practitioners, in Italy and beyond, were historians of Europe, who might take as their subject matter an extraordinary event, a thin slice of time, a small town or village, an exceptional individual who had hitherto escaped attention, or some or all of these combined: hence a story based on the inquisition of a sixteenth-century Italian miller (Carlo Ginsburg's *The Cheese and the Worms*, 1976); an intimate account of life in a small village in the south of France during the suppression of the Cathar heretics (Emmanuel Le Roy Ladurie's *Montaillou*, 1975); the mystery of a peasant imposter in sixteenth-century France (Natalie Zemon Davis's *The Return of Martin Guerre*, 1982); and, among more recent offerings, the story of a religiously-inspired kidnapping in a small village on the Dutch-German border in 1762 (Benjamin J. Kaplan's *Cundegonde's Kidnapping*, 2014).

What these and many other highly acclaimed works share – apart from a narrowness of focus (and, in the case of the four books mentioned, an engaging style) – is the exploration of some larger historical issue beyond the specificity implied by its title. So, the miller's story reveals the different belief system of common people, represented by the miller, and their inquisitors; *Montaillou* portrays in vivid detail the thoughts and actions of the village population; the story of the imposter exposes attitudes to the family, religion, property and the law; and *Cundegonde's Kidnapping* uncovers deep religious intolerance during what has traditionally been regarded as an age of Enlightenment.

This link between the particular and the general is usually seen as the distinguishing feature of microhistory. Individual microhistories, to be worthy of the title, must connect to larger historical themes, adding deeper understandings, confirming or challenging assumed patterns of behaviour, or structures of belief. Often they subvert a well-established paradigm. Their relationship with history on a larger scale has been likened to the juxtaposition in a Philadelphia museum of skeletons of a mammoth and a mouse, the mammoth representing a historical framework going back centuries, the mouse nibbling away at its foundations. Like the persistent rodent, microhistories present a threat to history. Mostly their impact goes largely unnoticed; but sometimes they have the potential to bring down the edifice.

There are other elements that microhistories often share – an emphasis on cultural attitudes, honour and belief, on people missing from the historical record, and on individual agency, the capacity of ordinary people to make choices and decisions that influence their own lives and the lives of others. Then there are similarities in method – a close reading of sources, a meticulous search for clues, an avoidance of anachronism, a readiness to flirt with fiction, and a self-conscious determination to reflect on the processes by which history is created (which is why you are reading these reflections now). The list could be longer; but none is essential for a work to be classed as a microhistory, except evidence of a microscopic vision and, in the view of most microhistorians, a desire to connect to large historical themes. The subject matter, in other words, is a means to an end. Not that the end is always in sight. As American historian Jill Lepore puts it, 'most microhistorians try to answer important historical – and historiographical – questions, even if their arguments, slippery as eels, are difficult to fish out of the oceans of story.'

By most of the above criteria, Cecilia Zoffany's story, as I am telling it, qualifies as a microhistory – though as I see no special virtue for a work of history to wear a label (except for the benefit of library cataloguers) or for a historian to be bound by a genre, I am content to let you, the reader decide. I mentioned earlier that her case probably had no influence on changes to the law relating to child custody, and no discernible impact on public attitudes outside Guernsey. Yet Cecilia's story might yet be significant for what it says about relationships among parents, their children and the state. How far that significance extends beyond the town limits of St Peter Port in 1825, again I leave the reader to decide – but only at the story's end.

Decree of the Cour Royale
3rd September 1825

On information given to the Court by the Constables of the Town and Parish of St Peter Port that Laura E. Horne minor daughter of the Reverend Thomas Horne, after having been placed under the supervision of the said Constables, has been removed, contrary to the Ordnance of the said Court dated 19th August 1825: In conformity with the conclusion of le Procureur du Roi, the Court in order to prevent the girl from leaving this island, has forbidden and now forbids all persons from hiding, harbouring, or assisting in the removal of the said minor outside this island on pain of exemplary punishment at the discretion of the Magistrates, and orders all public officers and others aware of the detention of the said minor to inform the said Constables immediately. And this Ordnance shall be published in the Market-place, and posted up in the usual places, in order that no person may pretend ignorance thereof.

The journal of Clementina Horne

The Prison, New-street, St Peter Port

Thursday, 8ᵗʰ September 1825

We have now been confined in this place for a week. After our arrest (how it distresses me to admit that term) when the constables had tried and failed to take Laura from us, we waited in gaol for two days before being summoned to the Court House. There we were each asked a long series of questions, intended chiefly to discover Laura's whereabouts. Mama responded to each question, 'I choose to remain silent', and I followed her example. Mr de Jersey was interviewed separately, and he too must have revealed nothing, thus confirming that our high estimation of his character is in no ways misplaced. The Jurats sent us all back to prison none the wiser from their inquiries, while we waited anxiously to learn what would happen next.

Yesterday we were summonsed before the Royal Court a second time, and we responded as we had done on the first. Mama had hoped the court might realise that future interrogation was in vain, and set us free; but alas, the Jurats have decided that she should remain in prison while *les Officiers du Roi* (as *le Procureur* and *le Contrôle du Roi* are always called) gather more information. They have released Mr de Jersey, having decided that they have no grounds on which to detain him. I too have been allowed to go free, though of course I shall not leave dearest Mama's side, except to see Laura. Perhaps the Court believes that I will lead them to her. But as I am at liberty to come and go at any time, I shall visit her only under the cover of night and when I am assured of not being followed.

Saturday, 10ᵗʰ September 1825

Last evening around 7 o'clock there was much commotion. We could smell smoke in the prison and soon heard the sound of fire bells. As I had been planning to visit Laura later in the night, I immediately sensed an opportunity and, heading out of town towards the Bailiff's Cross, made my way to M. de Campourcy's at Mont Durand. The streets were entirely empty, so I was able to pass unnoticed.

Although there was no moon, with the aid of my lantern I was able to find the house without difficulty, as Mr de Jersey had given me precise directions. There was a sign on the door, M. Louis-Prudent de Campourcy, professeur de la langue française. I knocked, and the door was immediately opened by an old lady, whom I assumed to be M. de Campourcy's housekeeper. She had evidently been expecting me, as she hurried me in without asking my purpose, then peered out the door in both directions to see if my arrival had been noticed. Then she ushered me downstairs to the parlour, where I discovered Laura saying her evening prayers in preparation for bed. She immediately burst into tears and rushed to embrace me – and I too was unable to hold back my tears.

Having been so long deprived of her Mama's company, she is understandably melancholy. I endeavoured to console her, telling her that Mama and Mr de Jersey were devising a plan by which we might escape this island and live without fear of pursuit. I hope the Lord forgives me this small untruth, for such a plan seems far from realisation. I also hinted that Papa, having witnessed our determination to remain with Mama, would no doubt become reconciled to our absence. By the time I left she seemed accepting of her fate and optimistic that her banishment would soon be at an end.

After about an hour, M. de Campourcy's housekeeper, who is a widow-lady by name of Mme Knight, interrupted to say that her master had given instructions that I should stay no longer, and bustled me upstairs to the entry door. Then, after looking again to ensure that there was no one in sight, she crossed herself and sent me on my way. Although severe in manner and appearance, she seems to have taken a great liking to Laura, and Laura speaks favourably of her in return.

On the way home, my attention was drawn to several posting-bills attached to shop doors that I had not noticed earlier. Holding my lantern close to one of them, I was alarmed to see that it offered a reward of £30 to any person who would deliver Laura into the hands of the constables. Mr de Jersey has since told me that notices have been distributed throughout the island and as far afield as Jersey and the Continent. I have begged him not to mention them to Mama, as they must surely increase Laura's chances of being discovered.

Sunday, 11th September 1825

As I had dreaded, our unhappy family has become the talk of St Peter-port. Today's copy of the *Gazette de Guernesey* contains reports of our recent appearances before the Royal Court and refers to the '*triste démêlés*' between Papa and Mama. I have not yet seen mention of our troubles in the *Star*, but I do not doubt the whole island will soon be gossiping about us in English as well as the strange French that Mme Lihou uses when talking to her neighbours.

Mama bears the indignity of her incarceration bravely, confident that the justice of her cause will prevail. As I think of the old men who are to judge her, I cannot be so sanguine.

At least our circumstances here are not so uncomfortable as I had first feared. Having never before stepped inside a prison, I had little idea what to expect. I am told that it compares favourably with the latest prisons in many English towns; and I know that our quarters, located in the gaoler's house, are far superior to the cells for criminals and debtors. Yet they are cramped and dingy, and as dark as a room in Bedlam, the only natural light coming from a small rectangular window at the rear of the room. Old M. Barbet, the gaoler, treats Mama with proper respect; and for last night's supper his wife brought us a ragout which I am sure was superior to the bread and potatoes served to the debtors. M. Barbet locks our door soon after sunset; but he says he will be honoured to allow me to come and go whenever I wish.

This morning I returned to Mme Lihou's to collect the last of Mama's clothing and pay her the little that was owing on our rent. There I learnt that Peter Lihou's carpentry shop in New-street had been burnt to the ground in Friday night's fire and that the whole family are all but ruined. He had insured the premises for just £100, far less than its value. His two apprentices have lost everything. I am very sorry for them all – it is salutary to be reminded that others have misfortunes almost as large as ours.

Tuesday, 20ᵗʰ September 1825

M. Barbet and his lady must be suspicious of my movements. Every evening except Sunday I ask him to unlock the cottage gate about sunset and beg to be admitted later in the evening. Yet they say nothing, and continue to treat us with the utmost kindness, so that the gaoler is more compassionate than the judge. Mama wishes to thank them for their goodness, but we have nothing to give them.

My visits to Laura are sometimes painful, for while she is usually affectionate, at other times she seems indifferent to my presence and more interested in conversing with Mme Knight or applying herself to her needlework. As she has now been confined for well over a month, I must make allowance for her moods, even when she so unfairly accuses me of not caring for her. On one occasion when she was crying inconsolably, Mme Knight descended the stairs and chided her and told her to beg the Lord's forgiveness for her ingratitude, which she thereupon promised to do. We are fortunate to be able to leave her in such solicitous hands. M. de Campourcy and Mme Knight adhere to the Catholic faith, which I believe to be little known on this island. As Mme Knight believes that Laura should devote herself to her religious studies on the Lord's Day, and that my visit might give offence, I have come to regard Sunday as my day of rest.

I time my visits to ensure that I do not interrupt M. de Campourcy's supper, which Mme Knight tells me he takes at exactly nine o'clock every evening. Mme Knight seems anxious to anticipate her master's every need, and to be fearful of the consequences should anything be wanting. Although I understand he spends most of his time in his study on the second storey, I usually chance upon him during my visits. He is an unmarried man, about fifty years of age, of middling height and slightly rotund. He tells me he has lived on this island for 16 years. Most of the time he speaks in French, enunciating his words with such force and clarity that I have little difficulty following his meaning. He evidently regards himself as a person of some importance, and appears to set great store on his own utterances, however inconsequential their subject matter. Hence, last evening, to Mme Knight: *La soupe, Madame - vous comprendrez que je vais accepter seulement les ingrédients les plus frais!* and frequent effusions in praise of French words and the French language. But I should not speak unkindly of him, as he and Mme Knight are doing our family a great service, and perhaps putting themselves at risk in doing so. And he speaks so warmly of '*son chèr ami*, Monsieur de Jersey', which of course endears him to me.

M. de Campourcy tells me he has received £10 to purchase food and clothing for Laura. I cannot doubt that this was given him by Mr de Jersey. How can we hope to repay that good man's many kindnesses?

Sunday, 9ᵗʰ October 1825

Still we wait in hope, but with little notion of what might happen next. Sometimes I wonder what my brothers and little Cecilia are doing in London and reflect on the monotony of my own existence. Yet my misfortunes are nothing compared to those of dearest Mama and Laura, who are unable to leave their places of confinement. Mama, despite all that is thrown before her, remains resilient, and Laura appears to have inherited her strong will. Yet she is often sulky and uncivil, and I have to look to Mme Knight to bring her into line. Mme Knight, like Mme Lihou, lost her husband on the Peninsular during the late wars and now spends much time preparing herself to meet him in the life to come. But she is a good-hearted woman, and with the blessings of her master spends many hours assisting Laura with her reading and writing and religious studies.

With the help of the money borrowed from Mr de Jersey, Mme Knight has purchased for Laura two new dresses and new body linen. This has allowed Laura to cast off her sailor's costume, which Mme Knight considered improper. Nevertheless, at Mama's insistence I have instructed Laura to put it aside in case it be needed on some future occasion. Laura's hair is also growing apace, which pleases her immensely.

Mr de Jersey continues to visit Mama frequently, though on some days he is prevented from coming by the pressure of business. M. de Campourcy has also commenced visiting Mama and me, which has been easily contrived by telling M. and Mme Barbet that he is coming to teach me French. As he had already been making regular calls on his friend Colonel Lang, who is in the debtors' gaol, his comings and goings will scarcely be noticed. He is an extremely voluble man and often amusing, though I do not think he intends to be so. Mama is always pleased to see him, as he provides earnest reports on Laura's studies. But when he speaks of some of the illustrious students he has taught and describes the benefits they have received from his teaching, it is hard to suppress a smile.

I have lately heard some unpleasant rumours about Mr de Jersey, but I cannot believe there is any truth in them. I have not told Mama.

Tuesday, 11th October 1825

This morning we were visited by Mr Drury, whom M. Barbet introduced as a clergyman lately arrived from England – though he was not wearing a cassock. He is an elegantly spoken man of middle age, with sympathetic eyes and courtly manners. He said that he was saddened to find Mama in her present situation and asked if he might be of service in any way. Mama thanked him for his kindness, and said that he could help most by praying that the Lord release our unhappy family from its trials and use his influence with the Bailiff and Jurats to allow us to escape this place. He responded modestly by saying that he had little influence with the laws of man but that he would certainly pray that God should look mercifully upon us. He promised to return within the week.

Friday, 14th October 1825

M. de Campourcy has been waiting on us regularly for my 'French lesson' – and while it is intended as a subterfuge, I believe his visits do indeed help me improve my conversation in that language. Although I am sure he has a perfect understanding of our language, he insists on conversing in his own. Each day he reports to Mama on Laura's progress with her studies, scarcely varying his information from one day to the next, to the effect that she is an obedient and serious girl, and attentive to the reading that he and Mme Knight set for her. From my own observation, she evinces more diligence than she has been wont to do in the past; but whether this is merely for the benefit of her kind tutors it is hard to say. With me she is often irritable and sullen, such that I am often tempted to slap her. I have stopped telling Mama about her moods.

Wednesday, 19th October 1825

On Monday morning, when M. de Campourcy was ushered into Mama's room he seemed more than usually pleased with himself. He announced that he had spent the night trying to think of a plan to rescue the child – as he invariably calls Laura – and now he believed he had one. 'I know a French lady', he said, 'a very accomplished young lady, who has long had a great passion for me; she is mistress of a school at Norwood, near London; she could take the child to a convent in France until you could join her.' Then he added: 'I know an old priest on this island who could accompany them, and I am sure that with my influence he will look after the child. In France, if a child is under the protection of a priest, there is no law that will touch it. Send me a letter mentioning the unfortunate differences between you and your husband, saying that it was all about religion, and I will show it to him. Tell him that you wish to become Catholics, as that will encourage him to take an interest in you.'

Mama was puzzled at first what to do, as she did not want to declare outright that she was not already a Catholic. But M. de Campourcy then said she must not expect that the child could remain at his house much longer, and that his plan would certainly ensure her safety; so she wrote the letter as he suggested, and gave it to him. He thereupon took his leave, saying that he would return soon.

The moment he had left, she expostulated: 'What have I done? I wish I had not written that letter. If Laura is shut up in a convent, I might be prevented from seeing her.' I said: 'Oh never mind, Mama, M. de Campourcy will be back again presently, and he may not see the priest.'

Mama scarcely slept during the night, and waited anxiously the next morning for M. de Campourcy's return. The moment he arrived she told him that she had changed her mind, and asked for the letter back, which he promised to give her. But the next day when he came he said that he had burnt it. We must take him at his word, though I know Mama remains uneasy.

This morning Mama had several visitors. Mr de Jersey came early, apologising that he had been less attentive than heretofore owing to the pressure of business; and next week, he said, he was obliged to travel to Jersey, where he expected to remain for several days. A little later Mr Drury came to pay his compliments and took with Mama a cup of coffee, which our gaolers thoughtfully provided. My opinion of him only improves on further acquaintance, and I am sure he wishes only to be of service. But as he was leaving M. de Campourcy arrived – and while I was unable to catch what passed between them, I believe M. de C. declined to take his hand. Upon entering the room, he said Bonjour, Madame, Mlle Clementine, and then, lowering his voice: Madame, I urge you to take particular care whom you choose as your friends – I will say no more! And, without brooking interruption, proceeded to comment on how meticulously he and his housekeeper were attending to Laura's instruction. M. de Campourcy is most anxious lest anyone overhear what he is saying; but he is ill-suited to conspiratorial communication, as every so often he resumes his usual effusive manner of speech, which he then suddenly cuts short when he realises that someone might overhear him. Unfortunately, my evening visits to Laura likewise yield little real information about how she passes her time; but I know Mme Knight pays particular attention to her reading and religious studies.

Thursday, 20ᵗʰ October 1825

The weather now is more congenial for extended walks – and as I felt able to leave Mama for a time, I arranged to meet my friend Lucy Mauger near the pier where Mama and Laura and I had stepped ashore nearly four months ago – though it seems much longer. Together we walked around the perimeter of the town, following a route similar to the one I had traversed with Laura soon after our arrival. Much of the scenery is now familiar to me, though some neighbourhoods I had seen only by night, on my way to visit Laura at M. de Campourcy's.

Lucy is just a year older than I am – she lately turned eighteen years of age – and she is exceedingly interested in everything around her, whether it be the grand estates, the botany or the geology of her island home, which she speaks about with much enthusiasm. Because her father is a newspaper proprietor, she keeps abreast of the latest reports of what is happening on the island, as well as the correspondence from London. During our perambulations, she told me that opinion here is decidedly in Mama's favour as to whether Laura should be permitted to return to her, and that many people – including her Papa – believe Mama should not be detained in prison a moment longer.

As I had asked her to inform me if our name appeared in the newspapers, Lucy told me we have been mentioned in the *Morning Chronicle* in London. When she said this, my dismay must have been visible, as she was reluctant to show it to me; but I pleaded with her to let me see it. It is a long column headed 'Matrimonial separation', and must have been written by someone on the island, though neither Lucy nor her father can imagine whom it might be. The writer reports very unfairly that Mama made Laura and me declare in the Royal Court that we could not bear the shock of parting from her, which is quite untrue, as our distress was nowise contrived; and he says that Mama played on the sympathy of the judges. He also observes, with what truth I cannot say, that officers had been despatched as far as France and England to search for Laura, which means that even if we managed to escape this island we still might not be safe. And he writes that the case 'has puzzled all the wisdom of the Court Royale, which has not yet decided in which way its fury is to be directed against this strange and dauntless woman'.

Of course, I shall not say anything of this to Mama. I fear that such reports will only increase Papa's determination to find Laura and perhaps demand that we all return to London.

I told Lucy that Mr Drury had visited Mama and asked her if she knew of any reason why M. de Campourcy should cut him: she nodded as though she understood, and said that people sometimes hinted that Mr Drury was overly partial to drink, and that this had caused him to be removed from a curacy in England – but she did not know if there was any truth in this story. There are many people on this island, she said, who are too ready to invent rumours, and many more who are too willing to spread them.

I shall ask Mr de Jersey his opinion of Mr Drury as soon as he returns from the neighbouring island. But until I see any evidence of excess or impropriety, I shall continue to think well of him.

When I called on Laura last night, M. de Campourcy descended to the parlour to tell me that Mme Knight had discovered her walking around the front garden of his house, where she might easily have been seen by a passer-by. Fortunately, he said, young children often came to his house for French lessons, and therefore she might not be noticed – but his neighbour, Assistant Constable Touzeau, might recognise her and demand of himself or his servant what she was doing there. Mme Knight, he said, was greatly alarmed by this prospect, so he told her that in the event of the Constable or his wife asking questions, she was to disclaim any knowledge of the child.

When I told Mama this, she immediately wrote to Laura thus:

'*My dearest*, – I live but in the hopes of still flying with you, my best beloved, to a happy country where we can follow our religion, and live without persecution. But it all depends on your paying strict attention to your GOOD FRIEND and the worthy woman to whom I fear you give so much trouble.

I have suffered loss of property, imprisonment, insult for you, and would suffer much more to defend you. Do not be wanting in yourself by imprudence and your kind friend will still save us all.

Adieu my darling.

I will write you in a few days.'

Mama has left the note unsealed so that both M. de Campourcy and his servant might read it. I am to deliver it to Laura tonight.

Sunday, 23rd October 1825

At last Mama has been summoned to court – but, alas, the case was postponed, as Mr de Jersey and Mme Lihou were out of the island. Mr de Jersey told Mama he had to visit Jersey on business, but I cannot conceive what took Mme Lihou away, or how, after the recent fire in her son's shop, she could afford to do so.

Mama has at least been able to choose her attorney. On Mr de Jersey's advice, she has asked M. Carré of Le Marchant-street, a young gentleman who is well known to be one of the most able advocates on this island. M. Carré has accepted without hesitation. This must surely mean that he thinks Mama has a strong case.

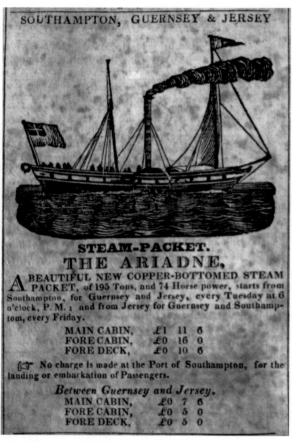

L'Independance, 6 August 1825.

Before the Cour Royale
Saturday 29th October 1825

The charge

The Officers of the Crown indict Mme Cecilia C.E. Zoffany, wife of the Reverend Thomas Horne, and a Prisoner in the Pubic Gaol, to be adjudged to such pain, punishment or corporeal chastisement as the Court shall deem fit, for having on the 31st of August or the 1st of September 1825, or thereabouts, either alone or with an accomplice or accomplices, withdrawn and taken away or caused to be taken away, Laura E. Horne, under age daughter of the said M. Horne and the said Mme Zoffany, in contravention of the Ordnance of the Court dated 19th of August 1825, &c &c. And in so doing the said Mme Zoffany has infringed the laws and disturbed the public peace.

⋙ On the rule of law ⋘

THE FIGURE OF JUSTICE that graced the Royal Court – blind-folded, with delicately balanced scales in one hand and a two-edged sword in the other – resembled statues that had decorated courtrooms through much of the world since ancient times. But the way justice was dispensed in Guernsey was distinctive and, save for the neighbouring bailiwick of Jersey, in many respects unique. And so it remains today.

The peculiarities of the system could be traced back, as island-ers were proud to say, to 'time immemorial', when the Channel Islands were a part of the Duchy of Normandy and subject to Nor-man laws and customs. In 1066, when the Duke of Normandy – William the Conqueror – ascended the English throne, Nor-mandy became linked to the English Crown. King John, however, lost his Norman possessions to the French king in 1204, excepting the Channel Islands, and these for their loyalty, or to secure their allegiance, were granted extensive privileges. These included the right to govern themselves in most matters and to maintain their own legal system, which was based on Norman law. In later cen-turies, these rights were confirmed by the English parliament; and they were jealously guarded by the islands' inhabitants.

By 1825 Guernsey's institutions of justice had been long estab-lished. There was a single court, which dealt with all matters, civil and criminal, and had the power to pass *Actes*, or ordinances; a presiding officer, the Bailiff (who was also the principal officer of the bailiwick); twelve Jurats, appointed for life, to decide on points of fact; and two *officiers du roi*, or Crown officers – *le pro-cureur du roi* and *le contrôle du roi* – who argued the merits of each case before recommending a verdict to the Bailiff and Jurats and, where appropriate, a punishment. Plaintiffs and defendants could choose one of six advocates, each well versed in Guernsey law, to represent their interests. The advocates argued their client's case; the Crown officers presented their conclusions and recommendations; the Jurats listened to the evidence and arguments; and the Bailiff (or his deputy), having consulted the Jurats one by one, summed up the case and delivered the verdict, applying a casting vote if the Jurats were equally divided.

The justice thus administered was based on customary law rather than a formal body of legislation. This meant that the law gradually evolved as an expression of customs and usages, which in turn responded to changes in the law. In considering the merits of each case, the court looked to customs and precedent, including ancient Norman law and its own more recent *Actes* and judgments. Customary law was by definition unwritten law. Yet, in seeming contradiction, from time to time it had been collated, most notably in the sixteenth century by an authority from Dieppe, Guillaume Terrien, whose commentaries on Norman law were ratified by the English Privy Council. This large volume, referred to simply as '*Terrien*', was cited with near biblical reverence by advocates and the officers of the Crown.

The legal men of Guernsey also looked abroad. The advocates had been trained at Caen, in Normandy, or Rennes, in Brittany, and so were intimate with French law, and they were well acquainted with Blackstone's commentaries on the laws of England. So when, as from time to time inevitably happened, *Terrien* was silent on any particular issue, and the court's own *Actes* and judgments offered no enlightenment, the advocates and Crown officers could look to other laws and precedents. And when no answers were to be found in any jurisdiction, they could resort with easy conscience to first principles and common sense.

This remarkable system was widely lauded. *A Guide to the Island of Guernsey* for 1826, published in St Peter Port, declared that 'In the administration of justice, hardly any thing can exceed the Royal Court of Guernsey. As a Court of equity it stands unrivalled. The magistrates are all men of fortune, and the very strictest integrity, always leaning to the side of mercy, patient and deliberate in giving judgment, and anxious to render even the prison as comfortable as possible for either the culprit or the insolvent.' And a London observer, having read Jonathan Duncan's *History of Guernsey*, published in 1841, rhapsodised that disputes were decided not by a mass of contradictory precedents and outmoded statutes, but by 'a sense of the moral right or wrong of the existing circumstances, as connected with that particular case'. Indeed, the island's jurisprudence shone out as 'a model for all the people on the earth'.

Others were not so sure. The aforementioned Jonathan Duncan, who had something of a reputation as a radical, wrote that 'With very rare exceptions, the jurats are elected from the mercantile class, are utterly ignorant of the principles of jurisprudence, and little versed in its practice; they usually pronounce judgment from a common sense view of the matter in litigation, as arbitrators or referees'; and, with some exaggeration, he remarked that 'there is no *law* in Guernsey', implying that this might or might not be a good thing. Some decades earlier, another disaffected historian, William Berry, commented on the absence of certain rights that Englishmen took for granted, including *habeas corpus*, which was 'as little known in Guernsey as the Turkish Koran'. There was therefore nothing untoward in Cecilia being detained for an indefinite period without trial. Likewise, when she observed (as we shall soon see) that the court was in 'the strange and uncomfortable position of being at the same time *judge* and *prosecutor*', the Bailiff, Jurats and officers of the Crown might well have wondered what point she was trying to make.

Berry, whose views were no doubt influenced by having spent time in the debtors' prison, noted the 'evident impropriety' of the Bailiff and Jurats being related to one another, which he calculated around 1815 to apply to at least eleven of the thirteen men sitting behind the full bench. Cecilia might not have known it, but when she attended the court on 19 August 1825, all seven Jurats who judged her (including Eleazar Le Marchant, Josias Le Marchant and Jean Le Marchant) were probably related to one another, as well as to the Bailiff and the Crown officials. Berry remarked that 'many evils and prejudices' might arise from such relationships. At the very least, they suggest a certain affinity of interest.

Berry also referred to the oddity of all trials being conducted in French, 'to the evidently great disadvantage of English suitors'. But English-speakers would have to suffer, as French, used as the official language of government and the law, was essential to maintaining and asserting the island's autonomy. The difficulties obviously increased as French and *guernésiais* yielded to English in the streets of St Peter Port; and the use of arcane terms rarely heard outside the courtroom made matters even worse.

Thus in 1825, three months after Cecilia's first appearance in court, Major Gustavus Hippisley, having lately been required to pay damages for repeatedly assaulting Richard Champion, Esquire, with a horse whip, complained in Court that *le Contrôle du Roi* had called him an assassin, and declared 'with warmth' that he should answer for it. The Comptroller responded by asking 'whether it was fitting that a public officer should, in the discharge of his duty, be thus repeatedly insulted in the face of the Court and the public'. Several of the Jurats 'appeared disposed to take up the matter rather seriously', until the Bailiff intervened, agreeing that the Comptroller deserved an apology. The Major, who in past years had vented his furies in the jungles of South America, said that he would apologise if the Comptroller admitted that he had acted improperly in using the term 'assassin'; at which point, the Comptroller explained that the French term '*assassinat*' was often used in legal proceedings to indicate an assault, and that he never supposed it would be construed to mean a murderer. Nor had he intended for one moment to wound Major Hippisley's feelings. The audience in the courtroom were so moved by the Comptroller's explanation that they burst into loud applause, drowning out the Major's response. Some of the Major's friends, no doubt realising that he was destined for prison, now urged him to apologise, which brought the ructions to an inglorious end.

Fortunately, Guernsey was usually a peaceful place, so that the court was rarely required to judge matters relating to life and death. As it happened, a murder had been committed a few days before Gustavus Hippisley's outburst, which probably contributed to his excitement at being called an '*assassinat*': but this event was, according to the *Star* newspaper, the first of its kind in at least fifteen years. Most of the Court's time was taken up with much lesser crimes: two Frenchmen found guilty of stealing small amounts of timber from a shipwright with the intention of selling it as firewood, sentenced to a month's imprisonment on bread and water, and banished from the island for six years; a carter convicted of maltreating his horses sent to gaol for a month, and severely reprimanded for his inhumanity; a soldier who insulted an officer sentenced to three days' solitary confinement on bread and water.

Just as the term *habeas corpus* was foreign to the Court's deliberations, so too it took no heed of another Latin dictum, *de minimus non curat lex* – 'the law does not concern itself with trifles'. Hence, a fortnight before Cecilia confronted her estranged husband in Court, the same courtroom was occupied with an action involving Ann Ollivier's cats. Late in the previous year Mlle Ollivier, who was famously litigious, visited England to attend a law suit in which she had an interest in order to watch over her counsel (and who, asked the Comptroller drolly, could blame her for such a praiseworthy determination?). Before leaving St Peter Port, she recruited young Sophia Martin to look after her three cats, promising to reimburse her for the necessary expenses. On her return several months later, she was distressed to find that two of the cats had died and another had been substituted in their place. Unsurprisingly, she refused to pay Sophia's bill. Sophia insisted that the cats had died of old age and sued, successfully, to recover her expenses. The case caused so much hilarity among the legal men that it was fortunate, opined the *Star*, that there were few observers in attendance, for it would have been difficult to silence the laughter in a crowded court.

But if the Court could chortle about Mlle Ollivier's eccentricities, any disobedience to its rulings or challenges to its dignity were no laughing matter. Jean de Jersey, as a member of one of the island's first families and brother of the Comptroller, should have known this when, during a case brought against him by the directors and treasurers of the Town Hospital, he challenged and insulted one of the Jurats. This was a case that Cecilia and Clementina would soon become painfully aware of; and although the nature of Jean de Jersey's challenge to the Jurat is unclear, the court had no doubt that his words amounted to a calumny, for which he should be fined and condemned, 'in conformity to the law as stated in *Terrien*'.

Whatever the rights and wrongs of any particular case, the authority of the law was paramount. As the Bailiff put it several months later, when one of those involved in Laura Horne's disappearance was standing before the bench: 'The Royal Court being the only tribunal of justice in Guernsey, it was to be respected, or anarchy would invariably follow.'

'Interior of the Royal Court, Guernsey', drawn by de Garis; lithograph by
C. Haghe; and published by M. Moss, Guernsey, 1829. A Court official,
perhaps, is describing the features of the Courtroom to a gentleman and
his lady and their young child. Although many of the furnishings and
decorations have changed, the Courtroom depicted in this lithograph is
easily recognisable today.
PRIAULX LIBRARY, ST PETER PORT

The journal of Clementina Horne

The Prison, New-street, St Peter Port

Sunday, 30th October 1825

The Court assembled yesterday to hear Mama's case. Soon after dawn, M. Barbet brought the intelligence that Mama was to prepare herself to appear at midday. At a quarter to twelve, the constables arrived and led her through a tunnel that connected the prison to the Court House. As I was not a prisoner, I was not allowed to follow, but was told to walk the short distance along Manor-road. It seemed that everyone was looking in my direction, some just gaping, and others muttering among themselves.

At the front entrance to the Court House there was a crush of people who seemed to be trying to gain admission. One of the officers of the Court recognised me, and shepherded me in through one of the side entrances. I was astonished to find the Court Room packed with spectators – and had not the kind Dr O'Brien saved me a seat in the second row, I might have been obliged to stand throughout the proceedings.

As Mama appeared and was led to the dock, everyone fell suddenly silent and it was evident that all eyes were fixed upon her. She was wearing the best of her three dresses, and although it is now frayed beyond repair, her handsome features and dignified bearing had not forsaken her. In ways that now I recognise too well, the Bailiff and the Jurats marched in and took their seats on the bench, and the Greffier read in French the ridiculous charges against Mama. Then *le Procureur du Roi* called one witness after the other, including everyone who lived in Mme Lihou's house when we had lodged there and the constables who were supposed to have been guarding us. Most of the questions were about what happened on the night Laura disappeared, and the *Procureur* seemed particularly inquisitive about Mr de Jersey's comings and goings. But as nobody actually saw Laura leave the premises, and as the lazy constables were chiefly interested in disproving their own negligence, I doubt whether he or the Jurats learnt much more than everyone knew already.

I had thought Peter Lihou was our friend, but he told the

Procureur that Mama and Mr de Jersey had many times told him that they would give him money for kidnapping Laura, and that Mama had offered him the enormous sum of £150 to take Laura to Cherbourg. He also asserted that Mama had given him a pound to sail to the nearby island of Sark and arrange for the gunner Joe Ithslewirst to conceal Laura until she was able to reclaim her. Then Mme Berryman claimed that, a week before Laura went missing, Mama had offered her ten guineas to leave open the shutters of her downstairs apartment.

I cannot understand why Mama's accusers are making these allegations, as I am certain there is no truth in them. Mama interrupted Peter Lihou several times while he was speaking, saying in English 'that's false' and calling him a 'shocking wretch', which caused several spectators near me to gasp. The Bailiff told her she was not to interrupt and that the orderliness of the Court had to be maintained – but how could she remain silent in the face of such calumnies?

After all the witnesses had been heard, the Bailiff asked M. Carré to address the Court, which he proceeded to do with great animation and conviction, referring to many law books and citing various cases, none of which seemed to me to have much to do with Papa and Mama and Laura, but which evidently impressed the men behind the bench. He insisted that there was no case to answer, as Mama and Papa had separated in England and Papa had allowed Laura and me to remain with Mama. It was therefore impossible that Mama could have abducted her on this island. Then he said that, even if it appeared that Mama had removed and concealed Laura, this would not be a crime against another person but rather an illegal act, in that she had defied an order of the Royal Court – and if there were to be a punishment, it must be a very small one.

In the course of his speech, M. Carré suggested that if anyone had kidnapped Laura, it was likely to be Mr de Jersey, who was known to have shown great sympathy for her and who had been seen several times at Mme Lihou's house on the night she disappeared. I was astonished by this accusation, as it was Mr de Jersey who had suggested that M. Carré was best fitted to represent us, and I assumed that the two men were friends. Mr de Jersey was not in the Court Room to answer the charges, as his trip to Jersey has evidently taken longer than he anticipated. I was surprised that Mama did not say something in his defence, and I asked her afterwards why she did not do so – but she told me not to concern myself about it.

By the time M. Carré resumed his seat, the Court had been in session for nearly five hours, and I feared that the Bailiff would postpone the hearing, as it was approaching supper time, and it was evident during M. Carré's speech that the audience was becoming restless. However, after briefly consulting the Jurats, he invited Mama to step forward and speak to her own defence. I of course knew what Mama would say, having suggested various words and phrases that might strengthen her argument. Although she was reading, she so obviously spoke from her heart that the Jurats listened intently, and the audience, which had fallen silent the moment she stood to speak, stirred not once during her delivery. She stood erect and composed throughout, and spoke with such feeling that no-one who heard her could doubt her sincerity and resolve. I was intensely proud of her and wished my brothers had been here to witness what seemed to me a triumph of persuasion.

Mama resumed her seat in silence. Then the whole audience, who throughout her speech had seemed to be holding their breath, set to talking among themselves and making such a hub-bub that the Greffier had to shout to restore order. Had they been asked to vote, I believe that every man and woman present would have urged that Mama be freed and that Laura be restored to her there and then.

But it was not to be.

Before the Cour Royale
Saturday 29th October 1825

Madame Horne's (Dame Zoffany's) speech to the Jurats

Gentlemen,

I appear today before your bar not with the appearance of a guilty woman, nor as a supplicant for mercy. I come here with the peace of mind that invariably proves a conscience beyond reproach.

The Officers of the Crown accuse me of contempt of this honourable Court. This is the essence of their charge against me. In a few words, I shall prove how far the accusation is unfounded.

In fact, Gentlemen, far from contempt, I hold your Court in the highest esteem. I know that you are here to administer the law, as representatives of our gracious Sovereign, with impartiality and justice. But I ask the respected members who make up this tribunal, is it reasonable to interpret a mother's refusal to be separated forever from her child as showing contempt for the Court? Is a mother not obliged to follow the law of God and Nature? Do not these laws uphold rights that are irresistible? If the King, my master and yours, demanded of me so cruel a sacrifice, I must refuse to obey!! ... You are too enlightened and too fair not to understand that I am only obeying the law that Nature has engraved indelibly in the heart of a mother, to never be separated from her child. *Maternal affection demands that she sacrifice everything rather than allow her child be torn from her arms. ...*

I have been accused of arranging the escape of my child. Ah! Gentlemen, suppose for the sake of argument that a divine and merciful Providence had granted my dearest child – the innocent object of my affection – a safe ark to carry her to a secure land, could you fairly punish me? Did you entrust me to look after her? No, Gentlemen, you know that by your orders I and my child were placed under police surveillance, day and night. ...

I have proved absolutely that I have not shown contempt for this Court; that I never consented to be separated from my child; and

Zoffany expresses the commonly held horror in Britain of the revolution in France and the breakdown of social order. 'Plundering the King's Cellar at Paris', oil on canvas, 1794.
WADSWORTH ATHENEUM MUSEUM OF ART, HARTFORD, CONNECTICUT

that I am not in any way responsible for her escape. I need not remind you that I have already suffered the pain of two months of prison, even before anyone was able to tell me what I was guilty of or before anyone gave me an attorney to defend me. Is there in this room any fair-minded soul who does not agree that the punishment has far exceeded the supposed crime?

I will not speak of all that I have suffered during these two anguished months of imprisonment. I will not mention the tears, the sobs, the cries of this young and innocent victim of a parent's love. My object is not to illicit your pity, much less your compassion. I ask for no favours. I seek only justice! Gentlemen, can I not flatter myself that I might obtain it?

Le Procureur du Roi

We have been instructed by the Court to pursue Mme Horne in relation to the case as it stands, and we are now fulfilling our obligation in doing so ... Mme Horne stands before you accused of contempt of court. It is not about forcing her to hand over her child and it would be contrary to the law if we were to force her to do so. ...

The facts are clearly proven. It is possible that Mme Horne had accomplices, but it is certain that she is guilty. Peter Lihou has testified that she offered him £150. It is also proven that she gave Mme Berryman money to leave the shutters open. She locks herself inside her apartment at 2 o'clock in the morning and the child disappears.

M. Carré averred that she has broken no law for which she could be punished. He is wrong: for it is declared in Book 10, Chapter 6 of Terrien 'that all sentences given by the Judiciary are executable and whoever resists or defies them is to be punished at the discretion of the Judiciary'.

Our task now is to fix a punishment. It is clear that Mme Horne has sinned, but she has sinned through affection for her child. She has already spent two months in prison. In view of these circumstances, I conclude that she should be condemned to two more weeks of prison, together with costs.

Le Contrôle du Roi

Gentlemen, every new question deserves a thorough assessment, especially when opinions are divided. The question now before us brings together these two elements: a new issue and a diversity of opinion; and as the recommendations I gave previously were not followed, I owe to the public, to the prisoner and to myself to establish the principles which have guided me in this affair.

When M. and Mme Horne appeared before the Court last August, M. Horne asked for the child, relying completely on his paternal authority. Mme Horne did not allege any single fact which could induce the Court to remove from her husband the authority that the law bestowed on him. In these circumstances, I believed I was obliged to conclude that the child should be handed over to the father immediately. I had the honour of explaining to you that any half measure would result in nothing good; that to allow Mme Horne to keep her child until the 1ˢᵗ of September was to give her the opportunity to take the child away, and could even give her the idea to do so. Besides this, it seemed to me that allowing her to keep the minor only several days would increase the pain of separation. However, Dr O'Brien having recommended that the child be left until the 1ˢᵗ of September with the mother, the Court believed it had to defer to his opinion. …

Much has been said about maternal affection and the child's attachment to her mother; all this is so natural that it does not need to be proven to be believed; but I believe that the rights of the father and the good of the child must take precedence over all other considerations.

The principles on which I based myself then are those which guide me today; they are held in the sacred words of paternal authority. *Yes, gentlemen,* paternal authority *is the corner stone on which social structure rests. Take it away and everything collapses, and there remain only ruins, the appalling ruins of anarchy and discord. The Romans were so convinced by this truth that there was a time when their laws granted the father the right to decide on the life and death of their children. In France, during the revolution, the ties of paternal authority were undone; the demoralisation began everywhere and when a better order of things allowed the government to work on a code, its first preoccupation was to re-establish these sacred ties, … to pay homage to the paternal authority. At the same time, the law maker set the punishment of imprisonment for any person who abducted a minor, and if the person abducted was under the age of 16, the punishment would be hard labour. This punishment perhaps seems severe at first glance. But when we remember that the loss of a minor is a perhaps inevitable consequence of his or her kidnapping, we sense the wisdom of the law maker.*

Let us consider the current case. Mlle Horne is the daughter of a respectable and rich father, and she belongs to several distinguished families. If she were with him, she would receive an attentive education, would have an appropriate marriage, and would live with honourable wealth. Today, how different are her circumstances: she lives at the home of a washerwoman, and was dressed as a boy! Alienated from the friendship of her father, she lives in poverty and runs the risk of dying in misery! And gentlemen, if the mother were to die in a foreign country! The possibility of this event makes me shudder!

I cannot attribute the kidnapping of this child to maternal love. No, gentlemen! This sacred fire shines in quite a different light. Maternal love will sacrifice itself for the well-being of her child; here the child seems to have been sacrificed for the hostility that the mother has unfortunately held against her husband. ...

And if kidnapping alone must be punished, then what must one say about a kidnapping carried out by the judicial guardian of the minor, by the same person who had promised a sacred obligation to the Court? Should she not be held in Prison until her duty has been fulfilled, until the sentence of the Court has been carried out? ...

I know that the Court does not exercise vengeance. But it must have its decisions respected and executed, and imprisonment for an indeterminate time is often the only means of reaching a solution: the judge has always used it against anyone who refused to testify to the Court, as well as anyone who, charged with a responsibility, refused to fulfil it – because there is no other way of executing the sentence. Imprisonment without any other form of trial until Mme Horne has fulfilled her obligation in delivering the child, seemed to me the right way to proceed. And the more I have thought about it since, the more it seems to me to conform to our laws and precepts, and the more I am convinced that the judge should have sent her straight away to prison, until the sentence was carried out. But the Court was of a different opinion ... Today, the charge against Mme Horne remains. I am therefore obliged to recommend a further period of imprisonment.

The Bailiff's verdict

We must judge on the basis of the charge presented to you. The parties involved are on this island; the father seeks to reclaim his child; the mother cannot justify her legal possession; and the Court judges that the child must be handed over to the father's custody. The Court indulged Mme Horne by leaving the child with her for several days, and Mme Horne abused this favour. It is clear that she is guilty and the Court must punish disobedience to its orders. ...

The Court condemns Mme Horne to fifteen days' imprisonment, together with costs.

The journal of Clementina Horne

The Prison, New-street, St Peter Port

Wednesday, 2nd November 1825

Yesterday Mama had one of her tormenting headaches, and to-day she is more dejected than I have seen her since we arrived on this island. I have endeavoured to lift her spirits by drawing up a calendar for the fourteen days until her release, and by crossing out each day as it passes. But she fears that, even after her sentence expires, our troubles will not be at an end, for we have yet to devise a plan to remove Laura to safety; and, she says, even when she is released the Royal Court might decide to lock her up again. Our debts now exceed £100, and we cannot depend on Mr de Jersey to save us from the debtors' prison.

To add to her anxieties, M. de Campourcy says he has heard that, as Papa has been unable to locate Laura, he is likely to

'The New Prison', drawn by W. Berry; lithograph by J.C. Stadler, in William Berry, *The History of the Island of Guernsey*, Longman, Hurst, Rees, Orme, and Brown, London, 1815. Cecilia was probably housed in a room in the gaoler's cottage, on the right.

return to Guernsey and demand that I accompany him home – he does not say the source of this story, so I do not know whether to believe him or not.

M. de Campourcy exhibits less warmth than heretofore. While he continues to behave very civilly, he several times reminded Mama that Laura cannot remain much longer under his roof. Although he has not said as much, I suspect he was exceedingly grieved that Mama declined his plan to convey Laura to a convent in France. He still attends for 'French lessons', though less often and more briefly than previously; and when I visit his house in the evenings to see Laura, he is nowhere to be seen.

I have heard no word of Mr de Jersey's return. I hope it is soon, for surely he will have sound advice on how we should next proceed.

Friday, 4th November 1825

We have learnt that Mr de Jersey returned to this island on Monday. I am surprised that he has not yet visited us, but suppose he is overwhelmed by the pressure of business. This morning his servant arrived with a note for Mama, which seemed to distress her – I asked her what was the matter? What does Mr de Jersey say? She answered: nothing of consequence, I will tell you later. She seems quite distracted, and unwilling to engage me in conversation.

Mr Drury called this afternoon, but Mama told M. Barbet to say that she was indisposed and unable to receive him. I made my usual visit to Laura and found her reading with Mme Knight; but I did not stay long, as I was reluctant to leave Mama alone.

Saturday, 5th November 1825

There has been an astonishing turn of events, which I can scarce comprehend, let alone decide whether it is for good or ill.

I knew that something was weighing on Mama even more heavily than usual – and today she told me all! Mr de Jersey has made a proposal of marriage – to *me*!

He wrote Mama from Jersey a week since, offering his hand, and saying that it would be best for us to marry in Jersey, so that no person might stand in our way. This, he said, would ensure my safety, which was currently in peril. And once it was achieved, he would take steps to remove Mama and Laura to France, just as soon as Mama was released from prison.

Yesterday he sent his servant Corbé to beg her answer. She responded that he might tell his master that he should come to see her in person if he wishes for a reply. This morning Corbé came again and Mama delivered the same response, rather more curtly. He also brought a letter from Mr de Jersey to me, saying that I could not have failed to notice how much he admired me and that he hopes, once he receives Mama's permission, to wait upon me in person.

Mama is as much astonished by Mr de Jersey's proposal as I am. She says that while we are greatly in his debt for his friendship, his behaviour does him no credit. But she does not absolutely say I should refuse him. Mr de Jersey is a man of means; and if I were to accept his proposal, our pecuniary difficulties would be at an end. He has certainly shown us great kindness and solicitude in the past, and given our present circumstances, I doubt that I could hope for a better match. How many gentlemen would be willing to marry a young lady whose Mama had been condemned to prison, however unjust the cause?

I cannot conceive why Mr de Jersey would wish to marry me, or why he would condescend to do so. He must know that I can bring nothing to the match, especially if Papa refuses to give it his blessing. Perhaps he regards me with genuine affection – and as I look back, I recall that from time to time he has praised my conduct and spoken gently to me outside Mama's hearing. But that seemed more as a father than a lover – or have I concluded thus because his age is nearer to that of a father than a lover? I suppose I should be flattered by his admiration, and perhaps would be so were it not for the manner it was conveyed.

I must sleep, as best I can, but will dwell on it tomorrow.

Sunday, 6th November 1825

I asked Mama what she intended to say to Mr de Jersey should he wait on her, but she merely said she would determine that if and when he came. I decided not to attend church, as Mr de Jersey – although he does not regularly attend himself – would assume that I would be there and might try to deliver me a message or engage me in conversation. But I contrived to chance on Lucy Mauger as she and her family were walking home after the service and arranged that we might meet privately this afternoon at the top of the hill, near Elizabeth College.

When we met, Lucy looked at me anxiously and seemed almost to know what I was going to say. We sat down on two large stones, out of sight and hearing of any person entering or leaving the College. I told her all that had transpired, and showed her the note Mr de Jersey had written me. She listened intently to every word, glanced at the note, sniffed contemptuously and cast it aside. Pausing for a long time, as if to gather her thoughts, she responded: I fear I am nowise surprised, as I have long suspected that Mr de Jersey is not the man you thought him to be. Then she produced from her bosom a long extract cut from one of the French newspapers, which she smoothed out on her lap and proceeded to translate for me.

It seems that many months before we came to this island a poor girl of this town named Mary Ann Jones had appeared destitute at the Town Hospital. When the Hospital refused to take her in, Mr de Jersey came to her aid and employed her as a domestic servant. Soon it appeared that the foolish girl had a lover and was with child; and as there were rumours that Mr de Jersey was the father, he took the precaution of making her write a certificate which said: '*I hereby most solemnly declare that I am not with child for Mr John De Jersey, so help me God*!!!'; which words, said Lucy, were written in English in the newspaper.

When the time approached for her confinement, she came again to the Hospital, which took her in and looked after her, as she said she had nowhere else to go. As the officers in charge of the Hospital (which is in truth as much a workhouse) had to ensure that the father should pay for the child's accouchement and provide for its upbringing, they tried to make the girl tell them the father's name. For a long time she said only that it was her lover (whom Lucy added was a young valet called Pierre Le Page). But the Treasurer of the Hospital did not believe her, and when he implored her to speak the truth, she threw herself at his feet and asked his forgiveness, sobbing: 'The child is Mr de Jersey's, it was he who made me promise it was my lover's'. So the

'… I contrived to chance on Lucy Mauger as she and her family were walking home after the service and arranged that we might meet privately this afternoon at the top of the hill, near Elizabeth College …' 'North Front of Elizabeth College, Guernsey', drawn by T. Compton; lithograph by [?] Haghe; and published by M. Moss, Guernsey, 1829. St James's Church is at the left.

child was baptised in Mr de Jersey's name.

The officers of the hospital then urged the Royal Court to oblige Mr de Jersey to accept his responsibilities as the father of a natural child. But *le Contrôle du Roi* said that he was angry that the case should have come to court, as it had been decided in a previous case that a mother was not a suitable witness, as she had an interest in the case, 'otherwise anyone would be at the mercy of all fallen women'.

I allowed Lucy to continue without interruption until she finished reading – and as she read, in her sing song voice which seemed so unsuited to the subject matter, I remembered that I had previously heard a rumour unfavourable to Mr de Jersey, but had dismissed it as vile slander. Then she said to me: Mr de Jersey is a dissembler; the whole island knows it, and I should have told you long since had I not feared I would lose your friendship.

I said to Lucy: did not the Court show that Mr de Jersey was innocent? Surely a foolish girl such as Mary Ann cannot be relied upon, for she would of course choose as father of her child a man of means and reputation rather than a servant? Lucy answered, perhaps; but then said: Oh Clementina, I beg of you to have nothing further to do with him. I responded: if I marry him Mama and Laura will at last be free and our problems will be at an end.

I was eager to terminate our conversation so I could comprehend the extraordinary story and all that Lucy had said, so I said thank you for meeting me, I must return to Mama; but as I wanted to think, I walked for some time through the parklands in the New Ground, my mind in turmoil.

On my return I learnt that dizzard Jeremie Corbé had again come to the prison, bringing yet another note for Mama, and saying that Mr de Jersey was not available to visit. Fortunately Mr Drury came afterwards and took coffee in the big room with Mama and Colonel Lang – and while he knows nothing of these transactions with Mr de Jersey, his presence offered Mama some small comfort.

I visited Laura as usual in the evening, but I fear my thoughts were elsewhere, so I could not bring myself to make conversation either with her or Mme Knight.

Monday, 7th November 1825

I have resolved to tell Mama that I will accept Mr de Jersey's proposal should she wish it.

Tuesday, 8th November 1825

Jeremie Corbé came as usual yesterday morning, bearing yet another billet doux. He is a shoemaker by profession, short and so vast of girth that he is probably unable to see his own feet. He has a grating, high pitched voice and an insinuating manner which is particularly ill-suited to winning Mama's favour. She sent him packing.

Later in the day, the kindly Mr Drury called on Mama and again offered his services. Evidently it is widely spoken of that Papa, frustrated in his attempts to locate Laura, will send someone to St Peter Port to bring me back to London. Everyone, including Mr Drury, seems to think that Laura is in France – so I can take some comfort that my nightly visits to M. de Campourcy have gone unnoticed. I have not even confided her whereabouts to Lucy Mauger.

The weather being clement, we were able to sit at the long table in the prison courtyard. Mr Drury whispered to Mama: Miss Clementina is at immediate risk. At that very moment Colonel Lang waddled over and, after bowing to Mama and to me, begged if he might join us. Mr Drury repeated: Miss Clementina is at risk; if you wish it, I can find someone who can accompany her to France, where you can be reunited the moment you are released from this place. Mama appeared alarmed by this proposal, and she was indeed astonished that Mr Drury should be so indiscreet as to mention it in front of Colonel Lang; but she responded calmly by thanking him and saying that she would think on it and give an answer tomorrow, meaning today. And there the matter was left to rest.

After they had left I asked Mama to tell me truthfully how she regarded Mr de Jersey's proposal of marriage. She said she had resolved to think no more of it until he presented himself to her in person instead of passing messages through his 'fat cupid'.

Then she asked me whether I could be happy in marrying Mr de Jersey. This was a question I had in truth given little thought to, as I had considered it merely from a prudential point of view, the benefits of such a union seeming to far outweigh the hazard of me being taken back to London and leaving Mama and Laura friendless and penniless on this island. I said to Mama: Mr de Jersey has proven himself a true friend, and we will ever be in his debt for his many kindnesses; and I believe he would make a good husband. I said nothing of my conversation with Lucy and the story about the servant girl, for I am not convinced in my own mind that he did wrong. I wonder though if Mama has already heard something of this story.

Wednesday, 9th November 1825

M. de Campourcy has come, red-faced and shaking with perturbation. He had heard, no doubt from Colonel Lang, that we had conceived a plan with Mr Drury for me to leave the island and feared that we would divulge his part in secreting Laura. Madame, he said, I urge you to have nothing to do with that man – he is not of our faith and he is not to be trusted. Although Mama tried to reassure him, he left muttering that he wished his heart had not been so tender, and that the child had been with him too long.

Mama was greatly distressed by this gentleman's visit, fearing that he might in his agitation hand over Laura to the constables. So she has written him to promise that she would never let slip any word that might harm him and to beg him to consider some means of removing both Laura and myself to France. I told Mama that we could both seek sanctuary in a convent without risk that we would be forcibly detained there – and that when she was released from prison the three of us would be able to start life anew.

Mama has also sent M. de Campourcy's servant an old gold cross that Grandpapa had given her, saying that she had no money but would recompense her for her troubles as soon as she had.

A letter from Mme Horne to M. De Campourcy

My kind Benefactor! ... *Rest assured, Sir, that I have that high sense of honour – that feeling of gratitude towards yourself. – The most devoted! – that I would prefer death, in its most horrible shape – sooner than by word create a suspicion! Feel therefore perfectly secure – that however I may endeavour to interest others! – to save my eldest darling – it will never be at the risk of injuring the noble minded french gentleman, who has preserved my youngest daughter! – No indeed Sir! – Clementina and myself would sooner perish!*

Ah Sir! – is there no place, that an unfortunate innocent mother, can for a few weeks, refuge her daughters? – Is there no convent they could be placed in, as pensioners, till I could join them? – My father was a Catholic, and that is a crime laid to my charge by Mr. H. – that his daughters are by me led to prefer the faith of my father! You Sir, are a french Gentleman! I rely upon your honour implicitly.

The journal of Clementina Horne

Friday, 11ᵗʰ November 1825

I have now marked fourteen crosses on the calendar that records each passing day of Mama's imprisonment. I showed it to her, reminding her that tomorrow we shall be free. But she said: your calendar says nothing of the near sixty days I have spent in this place before my trial, and nothing of the miseries and humiliations I have been forced to endure. And as the Court, for all their proclamations and the exertions of the foolish constables, have been unable to discover Laura, who is to say that they might not take it upon themselves to send me back to prison? And if I am indeed permitted to leave prison, where are we to go?

As I could not but admit the good sense behind Mama's anxieties, I returned to my book – until we were interrupted by a messenger from M. de Campourcy, saying that his friend M. Stewart, who lives near the brewery in Mansell Street, is willing to let us have a room for a short time at small rent. As Mansell Street is closer to M. de Campourcy's house than our former lodgings at Mme Lihou's, this will allow me to visit Laura with less chance of discovery. And Mama will surely be able to see her.

Jeremie Corbé came twice today, telling Mama that if she gives Mr de Jersey her new address, Mr de Jersey will visit her. Mama refused to give it – but of course Mr de Jersey will readily enough learn it from M. de Campourcy.

M. Stewart's House
Mansell Street
St Peter Port

Saturday, 12ᵗʰ November 1825

At last we are free! Constable Mellish came to the prison last night to say that Mama, having completed the sentence of the Royal Court, was free to leave today at 10 o'clock. As we waited for the bells on St James's Church to chime, M. Barbet and his lady came to bid us farewell – they have been so kind to Mama and me that I am sorry to say goodbye, though I of course hope I shall never see them here again.

'Town Church, Guernsey', drawn by de Garis; lithograph by C. Haghe; and published by M. Moss, Guernsey, 1829. People gossip outside the Church, while a woman and child wait for water to be drawn from the well at the right.

PRIAULX LIBRARY, ST PETER PORT

We walked away from the prison with our few possessions, and I led Mama along the high road, so as not to be noticed. Four gentlemen standing outside a shop on the other side of the road saw us and bowed to us and lifted their hats – I think they knew or guessed who we were, and certainly exhibited the utmost politeness. It is of course no matter now whether we are recognised or not, so long as my visits to M. de Campourcy's house do not raise suspicion.

M. Stewart's house is half-way up the hill, barely five minutes from M. de Campourcy's apartments. Having located it without difficulty, we were ushered in by his housekeeper and shown to a room on the upper floor. It is less commodious than our previous lodgings at Mme Lihou's, but so much more inviting than Mama's room in the gaol; and it has a small fireplace, which will be necessary now that the weather has turned colder. It should serve well enough for the short time we expect to be here.

M. de Campourcy has sent a message to say that I should not attend Laura this evening, owing to the risk of being seen by the constables, but that Mama and I might come to tea on Tuesday at 11 o'clock. Mama, having been separated from her dearest Laura for ten weeks, is desperate to see her, and said to me: should I not beg to see her earlier? But I said it was best to abide by M. de Campourcy's directions, and that the extra days will increase the joy of her reunion. So she has agreed to wait.

Monday, 14th November 1825

I had hoped Mama would attend church yesterday, but she was unwilling to expose herself to the town gossips, who would undoubtedly have their eyes glued on her. I therefore went alone and afterwards met Lucy Mauger, who said: please tell me you have declined Mr de Jersey's offer of marriage. I told her I would marry him if it meant that Mama and Laura and I could be free of persecution – at which she took my arm and said, no Clementina, only misery could result from such a union.

I cannot but believe that there has been some previous encounter between Mr de Jersey and Lucy's father for her to speak so ill of him.

I am tired from apprehensions about what will become of us

and what I should say to Mr de Jersey should he arrive at our
door. My courses have come early and last night I scarcely slept
a wink through worry. After dinner I told Mama that I had a
presentiment that I would marry Mr de Jersey, but she said that I
was not to think of such a thing, for while Mr de J. had been kind
to us, and we were greatly in his debt, his conduct of late has
been duplicitous and ungentlemanly. Mama has not mentioned
the servant girl and perhaps knows nothing of that story; nor
shall I mention it, lest it add to her ill-feeling towards him who
might yet become my husband.

It rained heavily last night, and the unpaved roads have become muddy, with water rushing down the drains in the middle.

Tuesday, 15th November 1825

Mr de Jersey has already discovered our whereabouts, for the
obnoxious Corbé arrived this morning, as we were preparing to
visit Laura, bearing notes for me as well as for Mama. My note
begged the favour of an interview, saying that a friend would accompany me to his quarters. Mama's said that she should see an
old lady who lives on the Catel road, who would be able to advise
her about my future. This time, rather than shooing the servant
away, Mama ordered him to wait at the door while she penned
a note to Mr de Jersey to the following effect: Sir, I do not need
the assistance of a fortune teller to tell me that you will not marry
my daughter, because I can tell you plainly you will not. You have
deceived us both. Your letters are as repulsive to us as is the great
fat cobbler who delivers them.

Then she folded the note without sealing it and with a wave of
her hand dismissed Corbé, who went snivelling off to his master.

As the time approached for us to visit Laura, Mama could
scarcely contain her excitement, asking many questions about
whether she had grown much taller, if she had suffered any further attack of the asthma, if her skin was much paler, and so on,
never giving me time to answer. Fortunately she did not know
the way to Mont Durand, or she would have rushed on ahead of
me – and several times I had to urge her to walk sedately, lest she
slip in the mud, and lest people wonder where we were headed
with such eager gait.

We crossed the garden and knocked at the door. Presently Mme Knight appeared and welcomed Mama, whom she had not seen before, with a natural and unaffected smile, and ushered us upstairs to M. de Campourcy's large sitting room, which was dark as the curtains were close drawn. M. de Campourcy, who was seated on his chaise longue, rose and bowed to Mama in his usual Frenchified way; then he said: Mme Knight, kindly summon the child, upon which Laura entered from the door that leads from M. de Campourcy's library, and curtsied to Mama. Mama said, my dearest girl, I scarcely recognise you, and approached to embrace her. But Laura stood motionless, without looking directly at Mama; and when Mama reached forwards and lent to kiss her, she moved back an inch and stood stiffly.

Mama was evidently astonished, as indeed was I, and said to her, come my dearest, have you forgotten me? For a time Laura remained silent – then she answered – and such an answer it was!! 'You do not love me, you will not let me go to a convent, but I am determined to go – you live among all the vanities of the world.'

Mama's arms, which had been outstretched to embrace her, gradually drooped to assume an attitude of pleading; and as if gasping for breath, she said: My child, what are you saying?

Laura remained motionless, then suddenly drew up her skirts and ran from the room; upon which Mama turned instantly to M. de Campourcy, and said accusingly: What have you done to my child? You have turned her against me.

M. de Campourcy, who had hitherto remained standing alongside the chaise longue, then moved swiftly towards Mama, saying angrily: *Madame, c'est une grande injustice!* I have done nothing to the child! She wishes to be with her father, which is her rightful place. M. de Campourcy's voice and manner were so alarming that I feared that he might do Mama an injury; and moreover that Mama might say something that would further inflame him. So I said: Mama, Laura is not well, she does not know what she is saying; and to M. de Campourcy: Sir, my Mama means no disrespect, she is shocked by Laura's ingratitude. Mercifully Mama seemed then to remember how much we were beholden to M. de Campourcy and dependent on his good will, so I was able to take her hand and lead her swiftly to the door and down the stairs. All the while, Mme Knight stood speechless, her hands clasped beneath her chin, as if imploring some higher intervention.

I led Mama slowly back to our lodging through drizzling rain, trying to avoid the prying eyes lurking behind every window shutter. Mama was desolate. It seemed as if she was dragging behind her a ball and chain.

Thursday, 17th November 1825

Mama has spent the last two days collecting her thoughts and trying to think what to do next. Mr Drury has visited, with soothing words but little sound advice.

Mercifully, we have been spared a visit from Mr de Jersey or his horrid cupid. I fear, though, their silence portends yet greater misfortunes.

A letter from Mr de Jersey
to Mme Horne

Friday morning, 18th November 1825

Madam, - It is not my intention to have any words with you on account of what is passed, for strong in my own integrity, such attacks pass by me as the idle wind, but as coming from an elegant accomplished woman, it would have been better had they been avoided.

I have matters of the dearest and of the last importance to communicate to you, which cannot be conveyed by letter. Time presses, a further delay may be fatal, in 48 hours it may be too late, it is not on my own account, but it is to offer to do you a most important and a last service that I now address you. I will wait on you between 7 and 8 o'clock this evening, to receive your final decision and instructions. …

With compliments to Miss Horne, believe me to be
Madam, Y.V.O.S.
John de Jersey

The journal of Clementina Horne

M. Stewart's House
Mansell Street
St Peter Port

Friday, 18th November 1825   Nearly four o'clock

This morning Mama received a note she so much dreaded from Mr de Jersey saying that he would wait on her between 7 and 8 this evening.

About midday we heard an urgent knocking at the door and who should appear but old Mme Knight, gripping a dark shawl tight about her face, and begging to be instantly admitted. She had come, she said, at great risk to herself, to warn Mama and me to stay away from M. de Campourcy's house. 'My master', she said, 'is in a d – d passion, and he is such a man in that way that I believe he would commit murder if anything crossed him'. Mama thanked her earnestly and pressed into her hands a silk scarf, which was all she had to give her.

We are of course now greatly alarmed. Mama is determined to refuse to see Mr de Jersey, and has told our landlady Mme Stewart that under no circumstances should he be admitted. But how can we rescue Laura?

Half past ten o'clock

As the hour approached when Mr de Jersey had threatened to appear at our door, Mama paced around the upstairs room holding her face in her hands, pausing often at the window to see if he approached. Eventually she said: we must call for Mr Drury; his wisdom and kindness of heart will surely guide us. He arrived within minutes; and when Mama showed him Mr de Jersey's letter, he said: I strongly advise you not to refuse seeing him, for your little girl's safety – nay, her life – might be in peril.

'Will you promise me', begged Mama, 'to remain in this drawing room, if I go down to see Mr de Jersey – for I am afraid of his violence, and shall not think my self safe, unless there is someone in the house who may assist me, if I scream or ring the bell violently?'

Mr Drury assured her he would remain here and give prompt assistance should it be needed.

No sooner had he spoken than we heard footsteps on the cobblestones; and looking down from the drawing room window, I recognised the familiar cloak and cane of our tormenter. Presently he knocked loudly on the door with his cane; and rather than wait for Mme Stewart to attend him, Mama – her hands trembling – descended to the parlour, telling Mr Drury and me to remain within earshot and take careful note of their conversation in case it should be her last.

'Bonjour Madame', he said – at which Mama asked him to speak in English. 'I am come from my friend Mr de Campourcy to desire that you will remove the child from under his care within forty eight hours, as he wishes to leave the island, and you having come to live so very near him, and Miss Clementina calling so frequently, he is afraid of discovery; otherwise he will be under the necessity of giving her up to the Comptroller.' Mama answered: 'It is not possible that he would be such a villain.'

He continued: the child will not return to you; she has sought my protection, and has begged that if I cannot take care of her I should send her to her father.

Then his voice softened, such that I had to strain to hear, and he spoke in the silken tones that I now know to be the voice of the Devil: despite all that has passed between us, I can still be of service to you. If you allow me to wed Miss Clementina I can retire with both your daughters to France, where Laura might be safely placed in a nunnery. If you do not accept this proposal (and here his voice again hardened), I will be compelled to deliver up Laura to a constable, who will hand her over to the Comptroller.

Mama screamed in response: 'No, Fiend! Never'; on which Mr de Jersey spat out the words: 'Dread my revenge!' and hastened from the room, just as Mr Drury, his cane raised ready to strike, rushed into the parlour, with me following close behind.

'Good God!' Mama exclaimed, her face contorted in anguish. 'What shall I do? What will become of my dear child?' And turning directly to Mr Drury, said: 'Cannot you, Sir, advise me on how my darling may be saved?'

'View from Clifton, Guernsey', lithograph by Day & Haghe, 1829. The Town Church and Castle Cornet are in the background. Mont Durand wound up the hill a few hundred yards to the south; like Clifton, it probably resembled a building site in the late-1820s.
PRIAULX LIBRARY, ST PETER PORT

Mr Drury, who seemed increasingly uneasy at the turn of events, answered apologetically: As I am a stranger on this island, I can think of no way of securing your daughter. But I know a gentleman, a native of this island, who has shown a lively interest in your misfortunes; his name is Mr John Brock; he is probably acquainted with some place of asylum.

Mama said: Sir, you have been so kind – could you please do me one last service? Could you find Mr Brock and bring him to me? Mr Drury immediately assented, saying that he would surely find Mr Brock at the Independence Club, and hurried off towards the market place.

In order to calm her nerves, Mama then requested that I make tea, which she was taking when Mr Brock was shown into the drawing room. His presence was instantly reassuring: he is a sturdy, well-built man of middle age, with rugged features, and seemingly able to defend Mama should any one attempt to assault her. I had seen him before – he lives at Upland Cottage, a fine residence with a splendid garden, not far from here. Oh Mr Brock, Mama exclaimed, 'I have fallen into the hands of villains.' She told him that she was miserable from Mr de Jersey's threats and letters, and that he had been there that very evening, threatening that he would deliver Laura into the hands of the constables if Mama did not consent to his marrying me, which she would never allow.

My little daughter, she said, is at this moment in the hands of her captors at M. de Campourcy's. I must go there to rescue her and I beg you Sir to accompany me.

Mr Brock, who was evidently shocked to learn that Laura was so close by, consented without hesitation, declaring that he believed both men had ungovernable tempers and that under no circumstances should she go alone. With that, Mama asked that I fetch her coat and light a lantern. I made as if to join them, but Mama turned to embrace me, saying no, Clementina, you must remain here lest Laura return alone – and with that they hurried onto the street and turned towards Mont Durand.

A scene

At M. de Campourcy's house, Mont Durand on
Friday, 18th November 1825

As Clementina did not follow her mother to M. de Campourcy's house, we must look to others for accounts of what happened there.

Six persons, at one time or another, were present in his apartments: M. de Campourcy and his servant, Mme Catherine Knight; Mr Jean de Jersey; Mrs Cecilia Horne and her younger daughter, Laura (dressed as a sailor boy); and Mr John Brock. M. de Campourcy's neighbour, Assistant Constable Davies Touzeau, also entered the residence, but too late to witness the main encounter. A crowd of neighbours, no doubt wondering what the ruckus was about, gathered outside.

Cecilia presented her testimony orally, in the courtroom. The other versions took the form of *interrogatoires*, or written statements presented prior to committal for trial.

Mrs Cecilia Horne

Mr John Brock called up at about ten. I told him everything that had happened, adding: "de Jersey and de Campourcy are two villains to cause me so much pain." I threw my cloak over me and we proceeded together as far as M. De Campourcy's garden door. Seeing Mr Jean de Jersey at the window, I said to Mr Brock: don't come into the house with me; but if I do not come out within an hour, come to my aid. I knocked seven times at the door and eventually the housekeeper opened it. I climbed the stairs and came into the parlour, where I found M. de Campourcy seated at one side of the fire and Laura at the other. They did not move when I entered. I told M. de Campourcy that I had come to fetch Laura agreeably to his orders, though I could not believe he would hand her over to the constables. He said that I would not allow my child to follow her wishes. "No Mamma," said the child, "I'll not go with you, I hate you, I detest you, you're not in the true religion, I'll stay with Mr de Campourcy and Mr de Jersey." My child, I said, have you already forgotten me? Can so short a time have weaned you from your mother? She said she wished to go to a convent in France; "that she was in the true faith, *and that she hoped to see us, my elder daughter and me, embrace the* true faith; *that she was sorry I was a devil, a heretic, and so on". I insisted on taking the child away. She fell on her knees. I opened the window in order to call Mr Brock, at which M. de Campourcy seized me by the throat, thrust my cloak into my mouth and nearly strangled me. I screamed* help and murder. *M. de Campourcy then himself opened the window and called out to Assistant Constable Touzeau, who lived next door. At that instant, Mr Brock came up, and went away almost immediately, accompanying Laura to my lodgings.*

M. Louis-Prudent de Campourcy

The mother came to me at about ten o'clock at night, holding a lantern in her hand, and having her body covered with a piece of woollen cloth tied under her chin. She was advancing very cautiously, when my servant called out to me, "Madame Horne." I requested the individual who was then with me, to retire for an instant, which he did. Mrs. Horne, on entering the apartment, said to me, with an affected tone "Bonjour, Mr. De Campourcy?" I answered "Bonjour, Madame, - take the trouble to sit down." She declined sitting down, but with a malicious smile, which appeared to be the harbinger of a storm, asked, "Where is my child?" "Here it is, Madam," I replied, turning myself away from her. "Is it true, Mr. De Campourcy, that the child wishes to return to her father?" "Madam, will you be so kind as to ask her the question yourself?" She accordingly put the question to the child, who answered it affirmatively. Mrs Horne then began to address herself to the child, urging her claims as mother, and representing to her the anxiety and trouble she had experienced on her account. She again repeated the question, "Do you wish to return to your father?" "Yes, Mamma," answered the child. At this, the mother became furious, and called the child a monster, viper, and other abusive epithets. The child fell on her knees, and clasping her hands, addressed herself to me, saying "For God's sake save my life, she will kill me." I endeavoured to compose the child, placing myself between her and Mrs. Horne. I remained in this position, my arms folded, and holding in my hand a volume of Anarcharsis, which I was reading when Mrs. Horne entered the room. She did not attempt to do any violence to the child, but turning herself to me, said, "Villain, it is the fruit of your advice." I answered that I had not given any advice to the child. But what was my surprise, when I saw Mrs. Horne coolly approach the window; immediately send forth cries, as if in distress; and finish by vociferating "Murder." Astonished at so strange a conduct, for which I had given no occasion whatever, I told her "Madam, why do you cry thus? If you continue, you will yourself cause your child to be discovered." She however continued crying, which induced me to open the other window, and to call myself to the constable Mr. Touzeau, my neighbour.

Mr Jean de Jersey

I was taking a glass of brandy and water with Mr De Campourcy about ten o'clock, when the servant came in and said, "Madam is coming." Mr De Campourcy desired me to go up stairs, that Mrs Horne might not see me, as he was determined to give up the child. I went to the bed-room, took off my shoes, and came to the top of the stairs. Mrs Horne made her appearance, disguised, with a lantern in her hand. … She then commenced by saying that Mr. John De Jersey had called on her that evening, and had told her that if the child were not taken away by twelve o'clock, it would be placed in the hands of the constables. Mr De Campourcy replied that Mr De Jersey could not have said such a thing. She said, "yes, he had;" also, that I told her that the child would not return to her mamma, but desired to return to her papa. Mr De Campourcy said, "yes, it is true, that the child wished to return to her papa", adding, "there is your child, Mrs Horne, ask her yourself." On which Mrs Horne asked Laura, whether it was true she preferred returning to her papa instead of her mamma. She asked that question three times, and the child answered, "yes, I wish to return to my papa," on which Mrs Horne flew into a violent passion and called the child a viper, and a variety of other names. The child then flew to Mr De Campourcy, caught hold of his legs and begged of him to protect her from her mother. On which Mrs Horne stopt for an instant, and then began screaming, and called out "Mr Brock! Mr Brock! Now is your time – now is your time." On which Mr De Campourcy said, "If you persevere to call out in that manner, I will call the consta-

ble." He then opened the window and called out, "Mr Touzeau, come here." He then went down the stairs saying he would go and call the constable. The child seeing him go, fled to me for protection, and Mr De Campourcy's maid-servant came up stairs with Mrs Horne, when Mrs Horne ran to the window and called out "Murder! Murder! Mr Brock! Mr Brock! Now is your time." Mr De Campourcy's servant told her, "there is nobody annoying you; you are disturbing the neighbourhood." I soon afterwards heard some voices which I apprehend were Mr John Brock's, Mr De Campourcy's and the constable's, on which I went into the bed-room with the child, and presently after the servant came and took her away. After this, I heard Mrs Horne calling out in the garden, "Where is my child?"

Mr John Brock

…Mrs Horne … requested me to accompany her to Mr De Campourcy's lodgings, and begged of me solemnly to promise her not to leave the gate, for she did not think she would ever come alive out of the house, and to alarm the neighbourhood if she was not out in an hour, which I promised. She went in, and on opening the gate, exclaimed, "I see Mr John De Jersey at the window," and added, "for God's sake do not fail me," which I promised not to do. She shut the gate and went in. I had not been long there when I thought I heard screams, and finding them repeated, I tried to open the gate, which I did by force. An artilleryman passing by at that moment, I begged of him to stay in the garden as murder might be committed, owing to the screams I had heard, and I rushed upstairs. Mr De Campourcy rushing past me, said 'Priez-là de ne pas découvrir son enfant' or words to that effect. In coming into the room, I found Mrs Horne in the greatest anguish, and not seeing the child "My God!" I exclaimed, "what has happened – where is the child?" A moment after, I felt a violent pressure, and a child dressed in boy's clothes, threw herself on her knees, crying, "save me." The child ran down stairs, passed through the garden accompanied by myself; and not having a hat I threw a great coat over her head, and took her to her mother's lodgings, and immediately returned for the mother, whom I accompanied home. … She seemed lost to every other sense but that of her infant, and kept crying, oh my child, my child!

The journal of Clementina Horne

M. Stewart's House
Mansell Street
St Peter Port

Sunday, 20th November 1825

It was after 11 o'clock when I heard hurried footsteps and Mr Brock and Laura appeared at M. Stewart's front door. Seeing only the two of them, I was terrified that something dreadful had befallen Mama. But Mr Brock quickly reassured me.

As I had feared, there had been a scene. But surely it could have been no worse than what followed in Mme Stewart's parlour. Laura, when she arrived there, was clinging to Mr Brock and gasping for breath, as she does during an attack of the asthma; and when I attempted to comfort her, she screamed – stay away from me! do not touch me! – and she refused to look at me. Mr Brock tore himself away from her grasp, and told her that he must go to fetch her Mama. Then he firmly took her hands and led her to a chair near the fireplace, where she continued to sob violently. Eventually Mme Stewart persuaded her to take a glass of cordial, and she began to calm down, but still she refused to respond to my gentle coaxing.

When Mama returned with Mr Brock, she rushed to Laura and endeavoured to embrace her. But Laura pushed her away and ran straight to Mr Brock and caught hold of his hand, begging him to take her home and saying that she did not wish to stay with her mother. Mama then seized her by the shoulders and shook her, crying out: what have they done to you? How can my child be so changed? And then, seeing that Laura was clasping something to her bosom, she said: what is it you have there? It was a book – and Mama recognised instantly that it was a Roman Catholic book. She seized it, and threw it into the fire, at which tears again came to Laura's eyes.

Again Laura appealed to Mr Brock to protect her; but Mr Brock said he could not do so: 'your ingratitude and unnatural behaviour towards your mother would be too bad an example for my daughter'. Then, turning to Mama, he said: your daughter has imbibed Popish ideas; the fittest person to correct them is her father, being a Protestant minister. She has already caused you much sorrow: I do urge you now to return her to her father.

Poor Mama was dumb-stricken by what Mr Brock had uttered, and although he insisted gently, I thought he had spoken very cruelly. She remained silent while he pressed home his case, showing how the Popish ideas had alienated Laura from her affections. Eventually Mama appeared to yield to the force of his arguments, and promised him to deliver up Laura to her father at the next opportunity.

This seemed to calm Laura. Eventually her wheezing ceased and we were able to lead her to our room, where we changed her out of her sailor boy clothes and laid her on my side of the bed. She slept restlessly through the night. Mama and I took turns sitting up beside her, to soothe her when she stirred, and to make sure she did not attempt to escape.

The following morning, when she woke, a change seemed to have overcome her. At first she remained silent; but after taking some breakfast, stood beside mother and fell to her knees, begging her pardon for what she had said at M. de Campourcy's, adding that she would not have acted thus but for M. de Campourcy.

Mama thereupon declared: my dear daughter, we can yet save you from those who would wrench you from me. And turning to me, she said: Clementina, you must take your sister secretly to Mr Brock's and she must remain there until I decide what next to do. No sooner had she spoken than she rushed Laura upstairs to our room and dressed her in a dress and cloak; I in the meantime wrapped my familiar cloak about me and tied my bonnet; Mama embraced Laura tenderly, and bustled us out the door. We made our way swiftly to Upland Cottage, where we discovered Mr Brock in his front garden with his workmen. He seemed astonished to see us; but before he had a chance to speak, I said: 'My sister is very sorry for what she said to mamma last evening. I am going to leave her, and my mother begs that you will come to speak to her'. Then, even without hugging Laura lest we draw further attention to ourselves, I hurried away. As I looked back, I saw Mr Brock take Laura by the hand and lead her into the cottage.

Mama has told me to stop scribbling, as nothing matters any more.

From *The Star*, Guernsey, 25th November 1825

Miss Laura Horne was found on Saturday morning at Mr. J. Brock's residence, Upland Cottage. It appears that she had been concealed until the preceding evening at Mr. Louis de Campourcy's. She was immediately delivered up by the Court to Mr. John Ozanne, who had a special authority from the father to take her to England. The Court were engaged yesterday, from noon until 6 o'clock in the evening, in examining several individuals who are supposed to have assisted in the concealment of this young lady. – They are to resume the examination this morning.

⊰ On evidence ⊱

WITH THE CHILD safely in the hands of her father's attorney, the Royal Court had no further cause to pursue the mother, and no appetite to do so – especially since public opinion appeared to be in her favour. But its orders had been defied and its dignity affronted. Plainly there were offenders, and they must be called to account.

So shortly after Laura had been discovered, three individuals were summoned to appear before the Court. Two of them, Jean de Jersey and Louis-Prudent de Campourcy, were charged with having removed, hidden and concealed the minor daughter of the Reverend Thomas Horne; the third, John Brock, just with her concealment. All three had defied the law and disturbed public order. All were to be 'adjudged to such pain, penalty, corporeal punishment, or fine, as the Court shall deem fit'. Each pleaded not guilty and each was granted bail. Brock declared that his role in the affair was entirely honourable; de Jersey protested, unavailingly, that he had already been imprisoned and then released for the offence of which he was now accused; and de Campourcy insisted that prisoners who were liable, as he was, to 'corporeal chastisement' had never previously been allowed bail, and that the charges were therefore illegal. This earnt him a sharp rebuke from the Bailiff, which set the tone for the coming trial.

Outside the courtroom, people were already taking sides, fuelled by exchanges in the press. On the day when the charges were laid, an unsigned article appeared in the English language *Star*, setting out 'the causes which led to the capture of Miss Laura H., and which may be deemed authentic, inasmuch as they are collected from those who have had a share in the drama.' This described in unflattering terms the behaviour of Jean de Jersey (identified, to avoid charges of libel, only by his initials), his threats to 'the unfortunate mother', and his proposals to marry 'Miss Clementina H.', which 'met with that undisguised contempt which they so well deserved'. It recounted the events at 'the house of Mr. C', referring to 'the mother's apparently stifled cries', her 'agonised feelings', the 'horror and dismay' expressed on her countenance; and then the moment when John Brock was compelled to surrender Laura to the police, 'Mr. B protesting against such arbitrary proceedings'.

Obviously the article was written by one or more of Cecilia's sympathisers – as well, perhaps, as Cecilia herself – and readers would probably have guessed at likely names. In case they were wondering, a letter written in English in the French language *Gazette de Guernesey*, endeavoured to set things straight. Its author was evidently Jean de Jersey, though it appeared over the nom de plume 'Truth'. Four persons, 'Truth' declared, had contributed to the statement that had lately appeared in the *Star*: an ex-clergyman who had been stripped of his gown for drunkenness; 'a notorious swindler', whose wife is an acknowledged prostitute and forger, now in the care of the Parisian police; a Guernseyman, 'a brainless blockhead', who has lately lost his wife; and the last, 'a woman, the daughter of an Italian, a Painter … a woman as celebrated for her *lying* as for her *drinking!*' The drunken clergyman was the Reverend Drury, the swindler Colonel Lang, the blockhead John Brock, and Cecilia was the daughter of the Italian painter (and while 'Truth' mistook Zoffany's birthplace, nobody could doubt whom he was referring to).

Louis-Prudent de Campourcy, evidently smarting from the Bailiff's rebuke, proceeded to make matters worse for himself by seeking to justify his conduct in a letter headed '*Au Public*' in the *Gazette*. He was, he wrote, forced by a series of misadventures to teach French to others, which made him too attached to the literal meaning of words – specifically, the threat of *corporeal chastisement*, which had deeply wounded his heart. As a stranger on Guernsey (though he had lived there for sixteen years), he was unaware that those words were appropriate to the alleged offence; and if he had protested too vehemently, he begged that his judges would put it down to the effects of warm-bloodedness. 'My duty', he declared, 'is to truth – my duty is to my character'. He would await the verdict of the judges, confident of their integrity; and in the meantime, he was suspending his course of lectures on French literature.

On the day of the trial, the Court Room was packed from noon until seven in the evening. After *le contrôle du roi* had very properly excused himself (his brother, Jean de Jersey, being one of the accused), the Court proceeded to enquire minutely into the events of the preceding three months, applying particular scrutiny to the contretemps at M. de Campourcy's house on the evening of 18 November. There were, as we have seen, various interpretations of what happened, differing sometimes in fact and often in tone, and exposing numerous inconsistencies. If de Campourcy and de Jersey were taking a brandy and water when Mme Knight announced that Cecilia was approaching, how did de Campourcy and Laura come to be seated by the fire when she stepped into the room? Did de Campourcy stand arms folded while Cecilia coolly approached the window to utter cries of murder, or did he thrust her cloak into her mouth and try to strangle her? Did Laura rush for protection to de Campourcy, de Jersey, Brock – or perhaps all three in succession?

There was obviously chaos and confusion: but, as with the affair from beginning to end, the evidence of what actually happened seemed largely immaterial. What mattered most to the attorneys and judges, as well as the watching public, was evidence relating to the character of the various protagonists, especially their moral conduct and religious beliefs.

Cecilia was not one of the accused; yet once again her manner and deportment came under scrutiny, especially accusations – aired by de Jersey in the guise of 'Truth' – that she drank to excess, and was intoxicated when she had confronted de Campourcy at Mont Durand – for how else could anyone explain her extraordinary behaviour? Such rumours, her friend the Reverend Mr Drury told the court, were 'utterly false and malicious'. Little wonder, said the Reverend, that Cecilia was agitated on the night in question: there was indeed a great change in her language and manner after returning from Mont Durand. But this, he said, was 'the uncontrollable excitement of a female deeply insulted, the vehement despair of a mother, threatened with the almost immediate loss of a child, for whose sake she had made the greatest sacrifices – and for whom I verily believe she would have sacrificed her existence'. Then, as if transposed from witness box to pulpit, he castigated those 'whose mouths are full of cursing and bitterness; upon whose tongues is the poison of the asp; who try to blacken and hideously deform the fair fame of an irreproachable mother, and sally with their pestilential breath the hitherto unspotted mirror of her reputation', before concluding with an apt quotation from *Macbeth*. The audience in the courtroom rose in acclamation, more perhaps for Cecilia than for her eloquent champion.

Louis-Prudent de Campourcy, already scarred from his courtroom encounters, defended himself vehemently, but to least avail. He told the court that he would not stoop to respond to the calumnies of his female accuser – as absurd as they were atrocious. He had lived on 'this enchanted isle' sixteen years, during which his conduct had been irreproachable, winning him universal esteem. His life had been one of peace and contemplation. But now 'the storm approaches, harmony flees, and the infernal goddess, landing her chariot on your verdant shores, has already withered the greenery. ... Now one can only see problems, plots and discord' – and so on, with florid metaphors, all of which the English *Star* chose to omit. Across the Channel, newspapers reported that de Campourcy had addressed the Bench with 'much energy', expounding on his respectable life as a professor, 'and a good deal of other French stuff'.

The Guernsey court, conducting most of its proceedings in French, could scarcely convict a man for Gallic exuberance; but it could certainly berate him for an offence against religious proprieties, such as an attempt to convert a child from the faith of its father, especially if the conversion was to the Catholic faith. Ever since the Reformation Guernsey had been resolutely Protestant. The local population was chiefly Church of England, with a leavening of Calvinism in the form of Huguenot ministers from France. In the late eighteenth century, though, other denominations had made an appearance – first Quakers, then Methodists and Dissenters – so that by 1825 there was a scattering of chapels as well as churches across the island.

Catholics, however, remained a small minority. Following the revolution in France, a few priests – including the former chaplain to the ill-fated queen Marie Antoinette – had escaped to the island and ministered to a small émigré population. But in 1825 there was still no Catholic church; and the *Strangers' Guide* for 1834 could declare confidently 'there are no native catholics', the Catholic presence on the island being confined to 'a few French and Irish families', and soldiers from the garrison. Nor were Catholics especially welcome: they were excluded from serving as Jurats and widely derided for their idolatry and subservience to ritual. While supporters of the Church of England were alert to rising pressures in the British parliament for Catholic Emancipation (which was achieved just a few years later), at the moment the Popish presence on Guernsey was little more than an irritant. Most islanders were happy to keep it that way.

So when stories circulated that there were plans to send Laura Horne to a convent in France, and it emerged that she had 'imbibed Catholic notions' during her weeks with M. de Campourcy, the court was understandably keen to probe what appeared to be a conspiracy. Jean de Jersey, asked if he believed that M. de Campourcy or his servant wished to make a Catholic of the child, said that he had 'not the least idea of it'; and that, far from there being any plot to send her to a convent, Laura herself had said she would rather go there than to either of her parents. Louis-Prudent de Campourcy flatly denied that he had suggested that the child be sent to a convent. And his servant, Mme Knight, testified that she had never heard her master speak to Miss Laura about Catholicism, adding that she did not consider him a good Catholic, as he often ate meat on Fridays. As to her own conduct, she swore that she had never given the child lessons in Catholicism.

Was it possible that Laura, and even Cecilia, were already Catholics? – in which case the alleged plotters could scarcely be charged with converting the child. Catherine Knight testified that Mme Horne had asked her, through her master, to lend Laura her prayer book; and she had sent her a small gold cross. (One observer in the courtroom remarked that 'the servant, we suppose by De Campourcy's instructions, tried very much to make it out a Catholic cross, but it was a plain cross of gold'.) Then there was the evidence of Cecilia's letter to de Campourcy: 'My father was a Catholic, and that is a crime laid to my charge by Mr. H. – that his daughters are by me led to prefer the faith of my father!'; and to Laura – 'I live but in the hopes of still flying with you, my best beloved, to a happy country where we can follow our religion, and live without persecution.'

There was also Cecilia's testimony, reported in one of the French language newspapers, that she had followed de Campourcy's advice and had written to an old priest, telling him that she and her daughters wished to become Catholics, this being the only way of persuading the priest to act as their protector. 'At first I did not want to say that I was certainly not a Catholic,' Cecilia admitted, 'but in the end agreed, and wrote the letter', before changing her mind and seeking to retract it.

The evidence of Cecilia's Catholicism is equivocal, as it often is in matters relating to religion, for it pertains not just to sect but to depth and manner of belief, all of which can vary over a lifetime. While a person's religiosity and spirituality might puzzle his or her contemporaries, the historian or biographer might find them all but impenetrable. Such is the case with Cecilia's father: while she described him, in her letter to de Campourcy, as a Catholic, Johan Zoffany, while once a devout Catholic, had in fact become a member of the Church of England before she was born; and he had later married Mary Thomas, 'Mrs Zoffany', in accordance with Anglican rites. His allegiance to the Established Church might have owed more to a recognition of where his bread and butter were coming from than to matters of faith. But how are we to know? In the absence of firm evidence, biographers and art historians have largely avoided speculating about his religiosity, even though his paintings are suffused with religious imagery. Perhaps the most persuasive conclusion comes from an art historian who has studied his paintings of the French revolution: 'Zoffany ... although a member of the Church of England was presumably still [around the time of the revolution] at heart a Catholic or, at the very least, sympathetic to Roman Catholicism'; and his paintings must be viewed in the context of 'a highly personal and creative response to religious doctrines'.

We might engage in similar speculation about how religion helped shape the events that culminated in Cecilia's appearance before the Royal Court in 1825. Was she, although nominally a member of the Church of England, sympathetic towards Catholicism, the faith her father had once professed? As her marriage to the evangelical Reverend Horne deteriorated, had she moved further towards Catholicism, taking her daughters – or two of the three – with her? In Guernsey, desperate not to lose her youngest daughter, did she agree to send her to a convent, before realising that she might never see Laura again?

And what of Laura? Was she torn between her parents' religious teachings? Since leaving her father's house she had lived almost entirely under her mother's influence, often chafing in the disguise of a boy. Suddenly separated from her mother, she found herself effectively imprisoned in the house of M. de Campourcy, a complete stranger. Alone and susceptible, did she fall under the influence of the devout housekeeper, Catherine Knight, embracing religious beliefs that distanced her from both her parents and the squabbles between them?

While all this is consistent with the available evidence, other explanations are equally plausible. A cautious historian can merely conclude that, as so often happens in reported struggles over the custody of children, religion played a part.

We can be more certain of the role of religion in influencing the judgments of the Royal Court, even though the officers of the court explicitly denied it. Louis-Prudent de Campourcy's advocate, M. MacCullough, responding to the allegations that his client had wanted to convert Laura to the Catholic faith, invited the court – probably unwisely – to consider whether this was a crime. 'Did the court in 1825 want to set itself up as a Protestant inquisition and persecute all those who did not belong to the established religion?' *Le procureur du roi* answered him directly: 'No person, he believed, could be a stronger advocate for religious toleration than himself'. Nevertheless, he considered it 'highly improper for any individual, in a country where there is an established religion, to endeavour to seduce a child from the religion of its parents'.

The Bailiff was of the same mind, telling the court that 'it was in a moral point of view' that M. de Campourcy's offences appeared greatest. He and Mr de Jersey had evidently hatched a plot to convert the child to the Catholic faith, and in order to give it effect had threatened her mother with handing Laura over to the police. But the parties had not been accused of these offences; for these they must be judged 'at the tribunal of their own consciences'. The crimes for which they appeared before the court were abduction and concealment, and for these alone they were to be condemned – in the case of de Campourcy, to a fortnight's imprisonment in the public gaol, together with all costs.

Jean de Jersey's reputation had preceded him, with the court appearing to agree with Cecilia that his proposal to marry Clementina was beneath contempt. There was also a suggestion that he had consulted a fortune teller, an old woman on the island of Jersey – and although he denied sending the seer's predictions to Clementina, he yielded that he had met her, which was sufficient to raise suspicions. *Le procureur du roi* was particularly critical: 'I am angry', he said, 'to see M. Jean de Jersey, the son of a distinguished magistrate who long sat among us, appear so often before the court. It is he who is the cause of all this. He removed the child, and his actions fly in the face of Justice.' *Le procureur* proposed, the Jurats concurred, and the Bailiff confirmed a month's imprisonment, likewise with costs.

Of the three accused, John Brock fared best in the courtroom. Yes, he declared: he had removed Miss Laura Horne from M. de Campourcy's house – but under what circumstances? On the mother's stifled cries of 'help!' and 'murder!', he had 'rescued a child whom I thought in a perilous situation, one whom I had never seen, dressed in boy's clothes, and without a hat'. Was there anything criminal in that? He had refused the mother's requests to take the child under his roof; and while Laura had been discovered at his house, he had made no attempt to conceal her. Perhaps most tellingly, he insisted that he had urged Mrs Horne to send Laura to her father, 'as the only fit person to drive such popish notions as she seemed to have imbibed out of her head'.

Brock, though described by Jean de Jersey as a blockhead, had acquitted himself well. While *le procureur du roi* suggested that he be fined, the Jurats, demonstrating their independence, determined that he should be released with merely a reprimand – though exactly what the reprimand was for remained unclear.

Thus the long day in court ended, the public gallery still overflowing. The Bailiff and Jurats withdrew; Louis-Prudent de Campourcy and Jean de Jersey were led away to prison; John Brock returned to his house in Upland Street, Cecilia and Clementina to their lodgings, and the spectators to their homes, clubs and coffee houses to make what they would of the day's proceedings. The evidence had been heard, the accused proven more or less guilty, penalties imposed, Justice served, and – what mattered most – the authority of the Royal Court had been confidently affirmed.

❧ On history & fiction ❧

O**N A RECENT TRIP** to Guernsey, I revisited most of the places
mentioned in this book – Glategny Esplanade, Smith Street,
Le Foulon, The Royal Court, Bailiff's Cross (where a large stone
marked with a cross stands, aptly enough, outside a funeral parlour, accompanied by a caption that tells the story that, in my re-
telling, terrified Laura Horne), and so on. In St Peter Port I strolled
along Mansell Street, where Cecilia and Clementina lodged with
M. Stewart after Cecilia's release from prison; continued to the end
of Upper Mansell Street; then turned right into Mount Durand, a
narrow one-way road, winding up the hill. I was looking for where
M. de Campourcy might have lived, well aware that there was no
prospect of identifying the actual house, but wondering roughly
how long it would have taken Clementina to walk there from the
prison and the two lodging houses.

As I rounded a corner, I noticed in a rendered wall to my left a
metal keystone, decorated with a bird, perhaps a great cormorant,
about to take flight, and two fleurs-de-lis; and bearing the date

Metal keystone, Mount Durand. Photograph by the author, 2016.

1824 – the year before the events of this book. Suddenly the details in Clementina's journal assumed a reality I had not previously been ready to give them. I could see her in the half-light hurrying up Mont Durand to visit Laura, glancing behind to make sure she was not being followed; and then Cecilia, holding her cloak around her head with one hand and a lantern in the other, rushing through the darkness to retrieve Laura from those she saw as her daughter's captors, with her intended protector John Brock puffing along behind. The keystone seemed to cement my story in reality. But had I become so absorbed in my subject matter that I could not tell the difference between history and fiction?

I have no evidence that Clementina glanced behind her to check that she was not being followed, or that John Brock puffed along behind Cecilia. I do know, however, from Jean de Jersey's reported testimony in the Royal Court, that Clementina visited Laura so often that Louis-Prudent de Campourcy feared discovery; and that John Brock accompanied Cecilia to de Campourcy's apartments. Did Clementina glance behind her? Was John Brock puffing? Does it matter?

Historians have long debated the relationship between history and fiction. Some have drawn a bold line between the two; others have recognised a grey area, conceding that history is part truth and part speculation. Some, in the last half century, have gone further, arguing that what happened in the past is inaccessible and that all history is essentially the historian's invention.

This is a risky business: historians might point to the complexity of their relationship with the past, but most readers expect history to be authentic. Just as visitors to museums are drawn by 'the real thing', readers of histories expect to be told stories that are true, or as near to true as the historian can make them; and when museum visitors discover that an object is in fact a replica, or readers learn that a story about the past is invented, they can feel disappointed, even betrayed. The historian must speak with authority, or no-one will listen; and the proof of that authority derives from reputation, acquired over decades, and obedience to a series of disciplinary rules and conventions. These are best represented in the paraphernalia of footnotes, which can be seen as the foundation of the historian's authority, as well as their Achilles' heel. Once reliant on written documents, historians in recent decades have vastly extended their sources, drawing on whatever evidence – archaeological, ethnographic, pictorial, oral – relates to their subject matter, applying to it the established rules of historical investigation, incorporating it into their footnotes, and defending its authenticity in the familiar way.

Occasionally they set aside the rules, at least temporarily, and experiment with fiction. Their purposes vary: to engage readers by drawing on the arts of the novelist; to strengthen their argument by presenting alternative perspectives; to link their narrative to contemporary issues; to fill gaps in the written (or otherwise verifiable) record, especially with regard to the secret thoughts and feelings of their subjects; to explain what cannot otherwise be explained. Sometimes the gaps are so wide that fiction seems the only recourse. Historians fill them with narrative or argument based on their creative imagination, borrowing perhaps from literary conventions, but always informed by whatever evidence they have been able to gather. Where imagination ignores or defies the evidence, the historian becomes a novelist; and while novelists, like historians, can speak with authority, they do not draw their authority from notes at the end of the book or the foot of each page.

For historians, recourse to fiction can be an indulgence or a necessity – and sometimes a necessary indulgence. Whatever their reason, they must take their readers with them, for it is the readers who will decide whether they can be trusted and whether they have anything to say.

Cecilia's story, as reported in the newspapers of the time, is full of detail, much of it confused and contradictory. I have tried to make it comprehensible by adding further detail about events and people, sometimes drawing inferences about what happened when, sometimes creating a character out of little more than a name. As I declared at the outset, much of the story is fiction – but while I have elaborated on the written record, I have never consciously distorted it. Notwithstanding its contradictions, the written record is the foundation of the story, and the keystone of this book's claim to authenticity.

Rounding the corner in Mount Durand, I was momentarily deceived into thinking the whole of Cecilia's story happened exactly as I have told it. Back home, with my typescript in front of me, I am reminded which parts are drawn directly from the record and which are my invention. Now is the time to come clean.

Every document, reproduced in italics – such as the arguments of the Officers of the Crown in the Royal Court, and the varying accounts of the scene at de Campourcy's apartments – is a faithful transcription, or sometimes translation, from original sources (though sometimes I have amended person, tense and punctuation to maintain consistency or improve the flow). Likewise, every sentence, word or phrase in inverted commas is a direct quotation. Other dialogue, lacking inverted commas, is either my creation or a rewording of statements delivered in court.

While I cannot specify the day on which Cecilia and her daughters arrived in St Peter Port, the main events that followed are well documented: the Reverend Horne's arrival, Laura's disappearance, Cecilia's appearances in court, her imprisonment, and Laura's eventual discovery. I have imagined the excursion to the Bailiff's Cross, drawing on well-known Guernsey folklore for the story Jean de Jersey told there. There was indeed a fire at Peter Lihou's workshop, but I can only guess that Clementina took advantage of the commotion to visit Laura at Mont Durand. The steam packet *Ariadne* commenced service to St Peter Port in 1824, but whether the Reverend Horne and Professor Brande were passengers I cannot say.

Every location can be found on a modern map, though occasionally place names have changed. Jean de Jersey (according to a map published in 1843) owned one of the larger estates in the Grange and (according to the *Strangers' Guide and Commercial Directory* for 1833) a timber yard on the northern outskirts of town, in New Paris Road; Louis-Prudent de Campourcy (by testimony to the Royal Court) lived at Mont Durand; and a Mrs Lihou, hairdresser and perfumer, appears in the *Strangers' Guide* for 1834 with a shop (to which I have added lodgings) in Smith Street in the Old Town.

With one exception, every person I have mentioned can be found in contemporary newspapers, books or archives. The main protagonists – Cecilia, Jean de Jersey and Louis-Prudent de Campourcy – all reveal themselves, and are revealed by others, in the court room and in the newspapers. Other characters are built on clues – the 'great fat cobbler', Jeremie Corbé; the defrocked clergyman, Mr Drury; the solicitous landlady, Mme Lihou – though as Lihou (the name of an adjacent island) was a common name on Guernsey I cannot be certain that she is the same Mme Lihou who appeared several years later in the *Strangers' Guide*.

The exception, Lucy Mauger (pronounced Major), is my invention. Clementina needed someone to inform her of Jean de Jersey's reputation; and who better to inform her than the daughter of a (genuine) newspaper proprietor? I also thought Clementina needed a friend.

Of Clementina we know little. The English newspapers that reported on the case remarked that she was 'a very fine and accomplished young lady', whose behaviour was exemplary: she 'never leaves her mother for a moment, and sleeps with her in the prison'. Later, when called to testify during the trials of Jean de Jersey and Louis-Prudent de Campourcy, she 'approached the bar in a modest manner. She is an interesting girl, and gave the same evidence as her mother exactly; and accompanied with similar looks of disgust upon Mr. de Jersey, and Mr. de Campourcy.' We know that she was a witness to all the significant events she described in her journal, though the journal itself is my conceit and indulgence.

And what of Laura? From the newspaper reports we learn that her distress was palpable, first, when she was threatened with separation from her mother, and then when her mother came to reclaim her. Perhaps she was in poor health: Cecilia's advocate, M. Carré remarked in court that the child had needed a lot of care, though latterly her health had improved considerably. In public, she dressed as a boy, a disguise that she had assumed – or that had been imposed on her – while the family was still in Jersey. De Campourcy reported that when she arrived at his house, delivering her mother's letter 'with trembling hand', she was 'dressed as a sailor boy', presumably a domestic variation of the garb commonly worn by cabin boys in the Royal Navy, and a forerunner of the sailor suits that became popular later in the century.

While it was not unknown in the early nineteenth century for women to dress as men, it was certainly unusual; and for a young girl to masquerade as a boy for a sustained period was surely extraordinary, if not improper. The Bailiff implied as much in his comment: 'she lives at the home of a washerwoman, and was dressed as a boy!' We can only guess how Laura reacted to her presumably enforced cross-dressing, her painful appearances in court, and her extended confinement. But guess we must, if only to remind ourselves that the child's responses to her predicament contributed as much to the eventual outcome as the actions of her parents or the decisions of the Royal Court.

With fragments of evidence and a modicum of empathy, I imagine that Laura abhorred her disguise and that it influenced her relationship with her mother. Is this the empathy of the historian or the novelist? I leave you, the reader, to decide.

⤳ Denouments ⤶

FROM THE LONDON *Times*, 28 November 1825:

'Miss L. Horne was delivered up to Mr. Horne by Mr. J. Ozanne, yesterday, Friday, November 25.'

For others, the story was not yet over.

Louis-Prudent de Campourcy, having been spared the indignity of 'corporeal chastisement', spent a fortnight locked in the town prison and presumably passed a gloomy Christmas closeted in his apartment. However fervently he might proclaim his innocence and high sense of honour, the decision of the Royal Court had assailed his reputation. As the island that had been his home for sixteen years held out no future for him, he counted his assets and prepared to leave. The last we hear of him is a plaintive notice in the *Gazette de Guernesey* requesting those to whom he had lent books to return them promptly to M. Gallienne, one of the town's auctioneers.

Jean de Jersey, after his month in gaol, seemed ready to return to the fray, the evidence of which is a column in the *Gazette* entitled 'On Slander', written by someone using the pseudonym 'Castigator'. It began: 'There is not a character among the human species more odious and insidious than the Slanderer'; and then, in florid language suitable to the subject matter, personified the monster who caused devastation in families, communities and nations. 'What enhances the guilt of the Slanderer is, that he often brings about his destructive designs under the most solemn attestations of undissembled friendship! *Love* is apparently on his lips, but the rankest poison is in his heart.'

Then 'Castigator' became more specific: 'Is there not, *at this moment*, some injured FEMALE bleeding in her *reputation*, in consequence of having been set up as a mark for this midnight assassin, at which to shoot his deadly shafts …'. And later, 'Perhaps he was *disappointed in his expectations,* and nothing short of the annihilation of the happiness of the individual who *could not* satisfy his request, would gratify his *insatiable revenge! –* Reader! Is this thy character?' If so, it was time to desist and repent, 'or the consequences will be fatal to thee in time and in eternity.'

Slander travelled fast and freely in St Peter Port. However likely it might seem, we cannot be certain that Jean de Jersey was 'Castigator''s chief or only target, or that Cecilia – even perhaps Clementina – was the 'injured female'. Nor can we identify the author or authors, beyond suggesting possibilities, including the Reverend Drury, John Brock, and perhaps Cecilia herself. We can be certain, though, from two later appearances before the Royal Court, that Cecilia was determined to defend her reputation.

On the first occasion she and two others – the Reverend Drury and Colonel Lang – sued the proprietor of the *Gazette,* Nicholas Mauger (father of Clementina's imaginary friend, Lucy), for publishing three months earlier the inflammatory letter signed by 'Truth' and countersigned by Jean de Jersey. That letter had also referred to a fourth person, John Brock, describing him as a 'brainless blockhead'; but he, after his bruising in court, was astute enough to quit the stricken field, having perhaps concluded that his association with Cecilia had caused him only embarrassment and trouble.

The court, after deliberating on relevant observations in the great law-book *Terrien* and in Blackstone's *Commentaries,* decided that the contents of the letter were indeed '*un libelle abominable*', for which Mauger, as publisher, must pay each of the injured parties £20, plus costs to the Crown. The unhappy proprietor, who had previously expressed his eagerness to apologise and his ignorance of the letter's meaning, was also obliged to publish in the *Gazette,* on three successive Saturdays, the decision of the court, to beg Cecilia's forgiveness, and to affirm that she was 'an honest woman'. As the *Gazette* reproduced in full the offending letter, the apology had the effect of telling or reminding readers that the drunken clergyman mentioned in the letter was indeed Mr Drury, that the 'notorious swindler' was Colonel Lang, and that Cecilia was the drunken liar.

A few weeks later, the same three plaintiffs sued the letter's author, Jean de Jersey, for damages. As the letter had already been adjudged offensive and defamatory, they might reasonably have predicted success. But the case was undone by a technical error and thrown out, with each of the plaintiffs being ordered to pay costs, which removed some of the gloss from their victory against Nicholas Mauger. Jean de Jersey, who had no more reputation to lose, emerged unscathed.

We might wonder why Cecilia, who had suffered so much at the hands of the Royal Court, risked having anything more to do with it. One motive, perhaps, was money, for she was probably in desperate need. No doubt too she was anxious to have the court uphold her reputation and deny Jean de Jersey's calumnies. But we must not rule out vengeance as motive. With no prospect of recovering her beloved daughter and nothing further to lose, revenge perhaps offered solace. It was as natural as a mother's love for her child.

Following the second court case and the three notices in the *Gazette* arising from the first, the Guernsey newspapers had nothing more to say about Cecilia and her troubles. At some stage, perhaps as soon as they could afford the passage, she and Clementina returned to England, though whether together or separately I cannot say. The only reference in 1826 to anyone by the name of Horne in the (incomplete) shipping records is an *arrival* at St Peter Port in December. Could the Reverend Horne or one of Clementina's brothers have come to fetch them?

We can at least trace the family in later years through records of births, deaths and marriages, and other official documents. The four sons of Thomas and Cecilia who survived infancy all moved to Australia and ended their lives there. Thomas, the eldest, who had accompanied his father and Professor Brande to Guernsey in a vain effort to persuade his mother and sisters to return to England, became a lawyer, government official, judge and politician in Van Diemen's Land, where he expressed radical opinions and mismanaged his finances, but was nevertheless, according to his biographer, 'competent and painstaking in his profession'.

Of the three girls, Cecilia, the middle sister who remained in Chiswick with her father after her parents' separation, married a military man, had two daughters, and died in Chiswick in 1876. Clementina, my co-narrator, married her first cousin Charles Dorratt, the son of her mother's sister, Maria Theresa, and a Royal

Naval surgeon, and gave birth to four children. Surviving her husband, she lived in Plymouth, Devon, during her later years, and died in London in 1880 at the age of 71, leaving an estate of over £600.

And what of Laura, the object of so much love and the occasion of so much misery? Returning to Chiswick and growing to womanhood in her father's care, she seems to have adopted the customary role of the youngest daughter, caring for him until he died in 1847, at the age of 74. Her father implicitly acknowledged her sacrifice in his will, dated a few years earlier: after specifying a small legacy to one of his sons, he asked Laura to distribute the remainder of his liquid assets in ways they had discussed, leaving the residue – which was no doubt considerable – entirely to her. 'I have been influenced', he declared, 'by no partiality or prejudice but solely by the desire of doing what is right in the circumstances in which I am placed'; and after expressing the hope that his children would all be satisfied with this distribution, he prayed that 'they may at all times be mindful that the only way to happiness is through piety and virtue.'

Laura had no children of her own. But fifteen years after her father's death she acquired a large family through marriage, at the age of 47, to Godfrey Tallents, a well-known and prosperous solicitor in Nottinghamshire. Like Clementina, she married within the family: Tallents' first wife was Ellen Horne, daughter of Laura's uncle Sir William Horne. Godfrey Tallents died in 1877, leaving a vast estate worth in excess of £90,000. Laura survived him by over a decade, residing at some stage in Lancashire with one of Tallents' sons and his young family. She died in Brighton, Sussex, in 1888, aged 73, leaving a respectable estate of nearly £8000.

Cecilia probably never saw again 'the child she valued more than her life'. Some time after leaving Guernsey, she moved to the vale of Llangollen in north Wales, a region justly celebrated for its natural beauty, and lived in the little town of Trevor Ucha. She died in 1830, aged 49, and was buried, according to Church of England rites, in the nearby village of Pontfadog, as remote from London as she probably wished herself to be.

She remained a shadowy figure. Just as many of Zoffany's paintings conceal as much as they reveal, so the written record leaves his daughter's portrait ambiguous and incomplete. That she was an adventurer, like both her parents, is clear; likewise that she was determined and defiant of convention, in ways that astonished and enthralled her contemporaries. But much of Cecilia's character, beliefs and motives remain a mystery, even during those several months on Guernsey, when her private affairs were exposed to the world. Mystery continued to accompany her to her resting place in north Wales.

The vale of Llangollen had long been a popular retreat from the cares of the world. Its best known residents for many decades were two aristocratic Irish women, Lady Eleanor Butler and Sarah Ponsonby, who were widely regarded as exemplars of ideal retirement. They were also noted for their unconventional behaviour. Decades earlier they had defied their families, rejected the prospect of unhappy marriages, and eloped to Llangollen, where they settled in a cottage they named Plas Newydd, or New Hall, on the edge of the township. Over the years they redesigned and elaborately decorated their house, created a fine garden, studied literature and languages, and cultivated rural simplicity. They had aspired to quiet seclusion. But their intense devotion to one another and unorthodox behaviour and dress, which included wearing men's beaver hats, inevitably attracted fascination and speculation, adulation and abhorrence. Their admirers were many, including the poets Wordsworth and Southey, the novelists Sir Walter Scott and Lady Caroline Lamb, and the Duke of Wellington, all of whom came to visit.

By the late 1820s, when Cecilia arrived in the parish, 'The Ladies of Llangollen' had lived together for about half a century and were well into old age – the elder of the two, Eleanor Butler, died in 1829. Cecilia must have known of them before she came. Perhaps they were a reason for her coming. Did they represent for her a retreat from the world of men? Walking the seven miles from Trevor Ucha to Pontfadog she would have crossed the River Dee at Llangollen and passed the lane leading to Plas Newydd. Did she sometimes call in on the old ladies and tell them about the loss of her child on Guernsey and her betrayal by 'wretched, perfidious man'? But again I am flirting with fiction. There is no evidence to connect Cecilia with 'The Ladies of Llangollen', apart from the coincidence of time and place and social class, which would have meant mutual friends.

Cecilia's story must end with my historian's feet firmly on the ground. The written record tells us nothing of her time in Wales, other than that she lived and was buried there. It does suggest though that her own unhappy future was foretold. A fortnight before the London *Times* announced that Laura had been handed over to her father, the *Gazette de Guernesey* published a poem describing a mother's anguish as she lost her child. Its author was simply described as 'A Young Lady'.

Could this at last be the authentic voice of Clementina, whose own voice (apart from a few words) has so far been my creation? If the author were indeed a young lady, I know of no other in Guernsey who could have written so intimately about the separation, or anticipated so precisely Cecilia's unhappy fate.

From the
Gazette de Guernesey,
10th December 1825

**A MOTHER'S FAREWELL ADDRESS
TO HER DAUGHTER,**
When separating at the Island of Guernsey.

WRITTEN BY A YOUNG LADY.

FAREWELL! Farewell, my Laura dear!
The child that I adore;
A piercing cry in my ear, –
We part to meet no more!

Ah! Laura, dear child of my heart!
What pangs do I endure,
To find that from you I must part,
When I thought you so secure.

Dearest treasure of my heart!
Look back and smile on me, –
Tell me I've done a mother's part,
And pity man's depravity.

Adieu! Sweet miniature of life, –
And may you never know
The pangs of an unhappy wife,
Or meet with man as foe.

O, wretched, perfidious man!
How could he us betray? –
A fond and trembling mother's plan:
What can the monster say?

When thy fond mother takes a retrospective view
Of scenes which now are fled,
Ne'er can she think that man is true,
But that philanthropy is dead.

Dearest object of thy mother's heart!
Tho' though art torn from me,
My wounded memory will smart
Whene'er I think of thee!

When thy father thee to his bosom has pressed
O, ask if he can find
The mother that has been oppress'd –
For loving of her child?

Vain thought! it must not be, – in me my Laura's dead;
The flattering scene is o'er;
My hopes are now ever fled,
And vengeance can no more.

Forgive me, Heaven! yet these tears will flow!
To think how soon my scene of bliss is past, –
My budding joys, just promising to blow,
All nipp'd and wither'd by one treach'rous blast.

Yet I do live! Oh! How shall I sustain
This vast, unutterable weight of woe;
This worse than hunger, poverty or pain,
Or all the complicated ills below?

I'll seek some lonely church or dreary hall,
Where fancy paints the glimmering taper blue;
Where damps hang mould'ring on the ivy'd wall,
And sheeted ghosts drink up the midnight dew:

There league'd with hopeless anguish and despair,
A while in anguish o'er my fate recline;
Then with a long farewell to parental care,
To kindred dust my wearied limbs consign!

But the last throb that leaves my heart,
While death stands victor by,
That throb, dear Laura, is thy part,
And these that latest sigh!

Notes

My account of events on Guernsey in 1825-26 is based chiefly on newspapers held in the Priaulx Library, St Peter Port, one in English and three in French. Their reports differ significantly in content and detail.

The Star: Guernsey Weekly Advertiser;
L'Independance: Journal Hebdomadaire;
Gazette de Guernesey;
Mercure de Guernesey et Publiciste de St. Pierre-Port.

Additional material appears in the *Southampton Town and Country Herald* (which appears to have been first to have received the story, but not first to have published it), the London *Times*, the London *Morning Chronicle*, and the London *Morning Post*. These reports were reproduced in other newspapers in Britain.

The decisions of the Cour Royale are held in the archives of the Royal Court in St Peter Port.

Introductions

4   Books on Zoffany and his works include Victoria Manners and George Charles Williamson, *John Zoffany: his life and works, 1735-1810*, John Lane, London, 1920; Penelope Treadwell, *Johan Zoffany: artist and adventurer*, Paul Holberton, London, 2009; Mary Webster, *Johan Zoffany, 1733-1810*, Yale University Press, New Haven, 2011; and Martin Postle (ed), *Johan Zoffany RA: society observed*, Royal Academy of Arts, London, 2011.

On the spelling and pronunciation of Zoffany, see letter in *Gentleman's Magazine*, vol 53, no 4, Oct 1783, p 849, which complains that Zóffany 'seems to threaten being the general usage'.

Christopher Hussey, 1930, compared Zoffany with Jane Austen: quoted in Amanda Vickery, 'Johan Zoffany, portrait painter of high society', *Guardian*, 3 Mar 2012.

Inadequate accommodation: Charles Tennyson, 'Johann Zoffany, R.A.', *Quarterly Review*, vol 227, no 450, Jan 1917, p 46.

5   'incontinence of the purse': Tennyson, 'Zoffany', p 42.

Zoffany on the French revolution: see William L Pressly, *The French Revolution as blasphemy: Johan Zoffany's paintings of the massacre at Paris, August 10, 1792*, University of California Press, Berkeley, 1999; and below.

'victims of self-gratification': Charlotte Louise Henrietta Papendiek, *Court and private life in the time of Queen Charlotte: being the journals of Mrs. Papendiek, assistant keeper of the wardrobe and reader to Her Majesty*, vol 1, R. Bentley & Son, London, 1887, p 86.

Mary Thomas: Postle, *Johan Zoffany RA: Society Observed*, p 261.

Bigamy: Sir Horace Mann to Horace Walpole, 10 Dec 1779, in the *Yale Edition of Horace Walpole's Correspondence* http://images.library.yale.edu/walpoleimages/hwcorrespondence/24/559.pdf [accessed 1 Jan 2016].

Quietly married: St Pancras Parish Register, 20 Apr 1805.

6 Papendiek on Mary Zoffany: *Court and private life,* vol 1, p 85.

7 'mischievous wit': Papendiek, *Court and private life,* vol 2, pp 138-39.

De Broke painting: I owe these observations to the Getty Museum's Object Details http://www.getty.edu/art/collection/objects/103264/johann-zoffany-john-fourteenth-lord-willoughby-de-broke-and-his-family-english-about-1766/ [accessed 1 Jan 2016]. On Zoffany and the conversation piece, see Kate Retford, 'From the interior to interiority: the conversation piece in Georgian England', *Journal of Design History*, vol 20, no 4, 2007, pp 300-04.

Colonel Mordaunt's cock match: Gillian Forrester in Postle, *Johan Zoffany RA: society observed*, p 271; also http://www.tate.org.uk/art/artworks/zoffany-colonel-mordaunts-cock-match-t06856/text-summary. I was first alerted to this painting's deeper meanings at the fine exhibition *Johan Zoffany RA: Society Observed*, curated by Martin Postle, at the Royal Academy, London, 2012; see also Pressly, *The French Revolution as Blasphemy.*

On gossip

9 Papendiek, *Court and private life*, 2 vols, 1887.

First biographers: Victoria Manners and George Charles Williamson, *John Zoffany: his life and works, 1735-1810*, John Lane, London, 1920, p xiv.

10 Zoffany's last will, 22 Apr 1805, reproduced in Manners and Williamson, *John Zoffany*, pp 297-98.

Mrs Papendiek on the Zoffanies: *Court and private life*, esp vol 1, pp 82-89, 184, 302; vol 2, pp 67-69, 137-39, 204-06.

11 'bitter things': Manners and Williamson, *John Zoffany*, p 134.

Horne from 1812 enjoyed a lucrative living as Rector of St Catherine Coleman in Fenchurch St: *The British Imperial Calendar for … 1840*, Arthur Varnham, London, p 252.

Separation agreement: *L'Independance* (Guernsey), 10 Sep 1825; *Morning Chronicle* (London), 12 Oct 1825. On marital breakdown generally, for a slightly earlier period, see Joanne Bailey, *Unquiet lives: marriage and marriage breakdown in England, 1660-1800*, CUP, Cambridge, 2003; and on separation agreements, Susan Staves, *Married Women's Separate Property in England, 1660-1833*, Harvard UP, Cambridge (Mass.), 1990, esp pp 177, 191.

The journal of Clementina Horne

14 Cecilia also suggested they had left Jersey 'afin de préserver ma petite fille des mains de ceux qui étaient à ma poursuite': *Gazette*, 10 Dec 1825.

15 *Peggy: Guernsey and Jersey Almanack for the year of human redemption 1826*, printed for N.Mauger and H.Brouard, Guernsey, unpaginated.

   Octavius Rooke, *Guernsey And Sark: Pictorial, Legendary And Descriptive. With a Glance At Alderney*, 3rd ed, L. Booth, London, 1859, pp 1-2, describes a rough voyage (albeit by steamer).

16 Sailor's suit: Clare Rose, *Children's clothes since 1750*, Batsford, London, 1989, pp 99-100; and Rose, *Making, Selling and Wearing Boys' Clothes in Late-Victorian England*, Ashgate, Farnham, 2010, esp ch 7.

   Landing arrangements: J P Warren, 'Guernsey in the Eighteen-thirties', *La Société Guernesiaise: Report and Transactions 1939*, The Guernsey Press, Guernsey, 1940, p 276.

   In fact de Jersey met Cecilia and Clementina walking next day: *Star*, 6 Dec 1825.

18 Narrow streets: Priaulx Library, unsigned article http://www.priaulxlibrary.co.uk/ articles/article/lamentations-de-damaris-poem-about-old-fountain-street.

19 150 steps: *Star*, 18 Oct 1825.

20 Hydrangeas: *Star*, 18 Oct 1825.

21 Property for rent: *Star*, Aug 1825.

   Jean de Jersey's business ventures: advertisement in *Gazette*, 3 Sep 1825. On the de Jersey family see John Jacob, *Annals of some of the British Norman Isles constituting the Bailiwick of Guernsey*, Part II, printed by J.Smith, Paris, nd, pp 182-86: Jean de Jersey receives no mention.

24 On treatments for asthma: Mark Jackson, *Asthma: The Biography*, OUP, Oxford, 2009, ch 2.

   French lessons: *Star*, Aug 1825.

26 The story of the Bailiff's Cross is told in various places, including *The Strangers' Guide to the Island of Guernsey and Jersey*, J E Collins, Guernsey, 1833, pp 21-23; Ferdinand Brock Tupper, *The History of Guernsey and its Bailiwick: with occasional notes of Jersey*, S Barbet (printer), Guernsey, 1854, pp 80-82; and Sir Edgar MacCullogh, *Guernsey Folk Lore*, ed Edith F. Carey, Elliot Stock, London, 1903, pp 242-47.

28 Large fortunes: advertisements in *Gazette*, Aug 1825.

   Lucy Mauger: Clementina previously misspelt her, as the name is pronounced 'Major'.

On history and pictures

30 For general discussion of history and art, see Ivan Gaskell, 'Visual history', in Peter Burke (ed), *New perspectives on historical writing*, 2nd ed, Polity, Cambridge, 2001. My approach to illustrations is greatly influenced by the late Joan Kerr,

who pronounced the dictum 'illustrations are documents, not decorations': seminar presented at the Australian National University, 16 Oct 1980 (copy in my possession).

'a dangerous book': Mary Webster, *Johan Zoffany 1733-1810*, National Portrait Gallery, London, 1976, p 19.

Lack of imagination: Kate Retford, review of Webster, *Johan Zoffany, 1733-1810*, 2011, *Journal of Eighteenth Century Studies*, vol 36, pp 153-54.

Zoffany and his condoms: for contrasting views, see Webster, *Johan Zoffany*, 2011, p 367; and Robin Simon, 'Italy, Old Masters & the Antique' [catalogue entry], in Martin Postle (ed), *Johan Zoffany RA: Society Observed*, Royal Academy of Arts, London, 2011, p 239; also Simon, 'Zoffany at the Yale Center for British Art', *British Art Journal*, vol 12, no 3, 2011-12, pp 4-6; and Edward Chaney, 'Intentional Phallacies', *The Art Newspaper*, no 234, April 2012, p 71. Art historians can be remarkably proprietorial: see Ronald Paulson, 'Zoffany and his condoms' [review essay], *Eighteenth-century Life*, vol 37, no 2, 2013.

32   Maria Theresa: see http://collections.britishart.yale.edu/vufind/Record/1668594.

33   Zoffany and his family: Webster, *Johan Zoffany*, 2011, offers the first title and Treadwell, *Johan Zoffany*, the second. In Postle's catalogue, *Johan Zoffany RA: society observed*, it appears as 'Self-Portrait with the Artist's Family', while Manners and Williamson, *John Zoffany*, call it 'Zoffany and his children'. Given that titles can influence later interpretations, perhaps art historians should indicate the provenance of their captions as well as the works that the captions often profess to describe.

An 'old family nurse': Manners and Williamson, *John Zoffany*, p 133.

34   Not the nurse: Webster, *Johan Zoffany*, 2011, p 596.

Option 1: Webster, *Johan Zoffany*, p 596; option 2: Treadwell, *Johan Zoffany*, p 421. Postle agrees with Webster. On art historians and guesswork, see Paulson, 'Zoffany and his condoms'.

Journal

35   Produce from Brittany: J P Warren, 'Guernsey in the Eighteen-thirties', *La Société Guernesiaise: Report and Transactions 1939*, The Guernsey Press, Guernsey, 1940, p 268.

Professor Brande: Frank A. J. L. James, 'Brande, William Thomas (1788–1866)', *Oxford Dictionary of National Biography*, OUP, Oxford, 2004 http://www.oxforddnb.com.virtual.anu.edu.au/view/article/3258 [accessed 9 Jan 2016].

Brande married Thomas Horne's youngest sister, Mary Anne Charlotte, in 1818: *Gentleman's Magazine*, Sep 1818; entry on George William Brande (1785-1854) in *Lachlan & Elizabeth Macquarie Archive* http://www.mq.edu.au/macquarie-archive/lema/biographies/profiles/brandegeorge.html [accessed 9 Jan 2016].

Surveillance by constables: Records of the Cour Royale, 19 Aug 1825.

37   Deeds of separation were of two kinds: legal separation could be granted by the

ecclesiastical courts on the grounds of adultery or cruelty; private separation agreements were not necessarily recognised by the courts. The Hornes evidently had a private agreement.

38   Cecilia told Dr O'Brien that she was willing to sacrifice her annual income and her father's legacy: *L'Independance*, 5 Nov 1825.

39   Description of Royal Court based on various sources, including *The Strangers' Guide to the Island of Guernsey and Jersey*, J E Collins, Guernsey, 1833, pp 84-85; and John Jacob, *Annals of some of the British Norman Isles constituting the Bailiwick of Guernsey*, Part I, printed by J.Smith, Paris, 1830, pp 142-43.

43   Clementina allowed to stay: Records of the Cour Royale, 19 Aug 1825.

      Cecilia's forthright response: *Gazette*, 5 Nov 1825; *L'Independance*, 5 Nov 1825.

On the history of child custody

44   Blackstone, *Commentaries on the Laws of England*, 1765-69, Book 1, ch 15 'Of husband and wife', and ch 16 'Of parent and child'; see also Tim Stretton, 'Coverture and unity of person in Blackstone's Commentaries', in Wilfred Prest (ed), *Blackstone and his Commentaries: biography, law, history*, Hart Publishing, Oxford, 2009.

45   Court of Chancery and the interests of children: Sarah Abramowicz, 'English child custody law, 1660-1839: the origins of judicial intervention in paternal custody', *Columbia Law Review*, vol 99, 1999; Danaya C Wright, 'The crisis of child custody: a history of the birth of family law in England', *Columbia Journal of Gender and Law*, vol 11, no 2, 2002.

      French revolutionary and post-revolutionary law: Suzanne Desan, *The family on trial in revolutionary France*, University of California Press, Berkeley, 2004, esp ch 3 and the useful chronology at Appendix II; Desan, 'The French Revolution and the Family', in Peter McPhee (ed), *A companion to the French revolution*, Wiley-Blackwell, Chichester, 2013.

      French customary law: Christopher L Blakesley, 'Child Custody and Parental Authority in France, Louisiana and Other States of the United States: A Comparative Analysis', *Boston College International and Comparative Law Review*, vol 4, no 2, 1981, pp 288-90.

      French excesses: Lawrence Stone, *Road to divorce: England 1530-1987*, OUP, Oxford, 1990, p 277.

      'then at the breast': The King against de Manneville, 12 May 1804, in Edward Hyde East, *Reports of Cases Argued and Determined in the Court of King's Bench: With Tables of the Names of Cases and Principal Matters*, vol 15, Butterworth, London, 1808, p 220.

      De Manneville case: Danaya C. Wright, '*De Manneville v. De Manneville*: Rethinking the Birth of Custody Law under Patriarchy', *Law and History Review*, vol 17, no 2, 1999 (with comments by Eileen Spring and Michael Grossberg, and a response by Wright); Abramowicz, 'English child custody law, 1660-1839', pp

1357-58, 1385-87; John Wroath, *Until they are seven: the origins of women's legal rights*, Waterside Press, Winchester, 1998, p 13.

46　No immediate change: See Wright, 'The crisis of child custody', pp 192-93.

　　The Westmeath case: Lawrence Stone, *Broken lives: separation and divorce in England 1660-1857*, OUP, Oxford, 1993, pp 284-346; and for a contrasting perspective, Maria Nicolaou, *Divorced, beheaded, sold: ending an English marriage 1500-1847*, Pen & Sword History, South Yorkshire, 2014.

　　Caroline Norton and the 1839 Act: Caroline Sheridan Norton, *The separation of mother and child by the law of "Custody of Infants," considered*, Roake and Varty, London, 1838; Wright, 'The crisis of child custody', pp 205-13. Limited impact: Wright, 'The crisis of child custody', pp 224-37.

　　Larger histories: a recent study sets parental alienation in a historical context; see Demosthenes Lorandos and J Michael Bone, 'Child custody evaluations: in cases where parental alienation is alleged', in Mark L Goldstein (ed), *Handbook of child custody*, Springer, 2015. See also Elizabeth Foyster, *Marital violence: an English family history, 1660-1857*, CUP, Cambridge, 2005, esp ch 3; and Joanne Bailey, *Parenting in England 1760-1830: emotion, identity, and generation*, OUP, Oxford, 2012.

Journal

49　Cecilia has Thomas arrested: *Star*, 1 Nov 1825; there were certain exceptions to the twelvemonth rule.

50　Rowbotham's boot shop: *The Strangers' Guide to Guernsey; containing its situation, extent and population*, J E Collins, Guernsey, 1834, p 137.

51　'a french gentleman': *Star*, 6 Dec 1825.

A letter from Mme Cecilia Horne to M. Louis-Prudent de Campourcy

52　Cecilia's letter: *Star*, 6 Dec 1825. In Guernsey, married women retained their maiden names, so that Cecilia is sometimes referred to as Mme Horne and sometimes as Mme Zoffany: see Jean Vidamour, 'Civil records in Guernsey', Priaulx Library website http://www.priaulxlibrary.co.uk/priaulx-library-new-details2.asp?ItemID=238 [accessed 15 Dec 2015].

Journal

53　Jean de Jersey's house: *The Strangers' Guide to the Islands of Guernsey and Jersey*, J E Collins, Guernsey, 1833, p 144.

54　Altercation at Mme Lihou's: *Star*, 1 Nov, 8 Nov 1825.

On small history

56　*Times*, 9 Dec 1825.

　　Population based on census figures for 1821 and 1827 in Gregory Stevens Cox,

St Peter Port 1680-1830: the history of an international entrepôt, Boydell Press, Woodbridge, 1999, p 163.

57   Census and *natifs*: Stevens Cox, *St Peter Port*, p 169.

Ancestral pride: *Star*, 18 Oct 1825; also *Dublin University Magazine*, 1846, reproduced as Priaulx Library article: http://www.priaulxlibrary.co.uk/articles/article/guernsey-its-present-state-and-future-prospects-society-1846;

Stevens Cox, *St Peter Port*, esp chs 6 and 7; and Rose-Marie Crossan, *Guernsey, 1814-1914: Migration and Modernisation*, Boydell Press, Martlesham, 2007, pp 185-89.

Huguenots and émigrés: Crossan, *Guernsey, 1814-1914*, p 122.

Increasing numbers of English: Stevens Cox, *St Peter Port*, p 94.

Channel islands dialects: William Berry, *The history of the island of Guernsey*, Longman, Hurst, Rees, Orme, and Brown [etc.], London, 1815, p 195; Crossan, *Guernsey, 1814-1914*, p 243; Louisa Lane Clarke, 'Guernsey French', extract from 1841 *Guide* reproduced by Priaulx Library http://www.priaulxlibrary.co.uk/articles/article/guernsey-french [accessed 22 Feb 2017].

Fashionable young ladies: *Star*, 18 Oct 1825.

English manners: Crossan, *Guernsey, 1814-1914*, pp 236-41.

Newspapers: Jonathan Duncan (ed), *The Guernsey and Jersey Magazine*, M.Moss and others, Guernsey, 1836, p 53; Ferdinand Brock Tupper, *The History of Guernsey and its Bailiwick*, S.Barbet (printer), Guernsey, 1854, p 432; Crossan, *Guernsey, 1814-1914*, pp 236-37.

59   Stevens Cox, *St Peter Port*, discusses at length how the town functioned as an entrepôt.

Shipping: *Guide to the Island of Guernsey*, Guernsey, 1826, pp 47-48; advertisements in the *Star* and other newspapers.

Hotels and lodgings: *Star*, 18 Oct 1825.

Café Français: J. P. Cochrane, *A Guide to the Island of Guernsey*, 1826, p 7.

On small island cultures, specifically Guernsey, see Gregory Stevens Cox, 'Islomania and Guernsey', *Refereed paper from the Sixth International Small Island Cultures Conference*, Guernsey, June 2010, http://sicri-network.org/ISIC6/c.%20ISIC6P%20Cox.pdf [accessed 1 Jun 2015].

60   For critiques of 'turns', see 'AHR Forum: Historiographic "Turns" in Critical Perspective', *American Historical Review*, vol.117, no.3, Jun 2012.

For a succinct and wide-ranging outline of microhistory, see Peter Burke, 'The Invention of Micro-history', *Rivista di Storia Economica*, vol.XXIV, no.3, Dec 2008, pp 259-73. See also Edward Muir and Guido Ruggiero (eds), *Microhistory and the lost peoples of Europe*, Johns Hopkins UP, Baltimore, 1991, esp Muir's 'Introduction: observing trifles'; Giovanni Levi, 'On Microhistory', in Burke (ed), *New Perspectives in Historical Writing*, 2nd ed, Polity Press, Cambridge, 2001; Levi, 'Microhistory and the Recovery of Complexity', in Susanna Fellman and Marjatta Rahikainen (eds), *Historical knowledge in quest of theory, method and evidence*, Cambridge Scholars,

Newcastle upon Tyne, 2012 (Levi takes issue with Burke); Carlo Ginzburg, *Threads and traces: true, false, fictive*, University of California Press, Berkeley, 2012, esp ch 14, 'Microhistory: two or three things that I know about it'; and Sigurður Gylfi Magnússon and István M. Szijártó, *What is microhistory? theory and practice*, Routledge, London, 2013.

61 Philadelphia museum: Florike Egmond and Peter Mason, *The mammoth and the mouse: microhistory and morphology*, Johns Hopkins UP, Baltimore, 1997, p 1.

62 Slippery as eels: Jill Lepore, 'Historians Who Love Too Much: Reflections on Microhistory and Biography', *Journal of American history*, vol.88, no.1, Jun 2001, p 133. Like other historical genres, microhistory has its critics. Some say that little can come of studying the trivial; others that too much is often made of too little. The challenge, as critics and supporters agree, is to show how the growing corpus of microhistorical studies illuminates larger structures. Cultural historian Peter Burke wondered in 2001 whether microhistory had yielded to the law of diminishing returns. Was it possible, wrote Burke, to link the experiences with structures, face to face relationships with the social system, the local with the global? 'If this question is not taken seriously, microhistory might become a kind of escapism, an acceptance of a fragmented world rather than an attempt to make sense of it.' 'The Microhistory Debate', in Burke (ed), *New Perspectives in Historical Writing*, pp 115-17. For more recent reflections on the relationship between micro- and macro-history see Eva Bischoff, 'Experiences, actors, spaces: dimensions of settler colonialism in transnational perspective', *Settler Colonial Studies*, 2015.

Decree of the Cour Royale

63 Decree translated from Records of the Cour Royale, 3 Sep 1825; and *Star*, 6 Dec 1825.

Journal

64 Remaining silent: *Star*, 1 Nov 1825.
   Fire: *Mercure*, 10 Sep 1825; *Star*, 13 Sep 1825.

65 £30 reward offered by Thomas Horne jnr: *L'Independance*, 10 Sep 1825; handbills: *Morning Chronicle*, 4 Oct 1825.

66 Guernsey prison: *Guide to the Island of Guernsey*, 1826, p 24.

70 De Campourcy's plan: story and quotations based on several, sometimes contradictory, newspaper reports and translations: *Star*, 6 Dec 1825; *Gazette*, 10 Dec 1825; *L'Independance*, 10 Dec 1825; *Morning Post*, 13 Dec 1825.

72 *Morning Post*, 12 Oct 1825.

73 Cecilia's undated letter to Laura: *Star*, 20 Dec 1825.

Before the Cour Royale

75 Condensed and amended from Court Records and *Star*, 1 Nov 1825; see also *Star*, 29 Nov 1825, for translation of later indictment of Jean de Jersey.

On the rule of law

76 On Guernsey law see Gordon Dawes, *Laws of Guernsey*, Hart, Oxford, 2003, esp chs 1 ('Sources of Guernsey Law and the Force of Precedent') and 2 ('The Constitution of the Bailiwick').

'time immemorial': Daniel de Lisle Brock, Bailiff of Guernsey, and others to Lord Melbourne, 13 Aug 1832, reproduced in Jonathan Duncan, *The History of Guernsey; with occasional notices of Jersey, Alderney, and Sark, and biographical sketches*, Longman, Brown, Green, and Longmans, London, 1841, p 215.

Descriptions of the legal system include William Berry, *The history of the island of Guernsey*, esp pp 193-95; Duncan, *The History of Guernsey*, esp pp 452-71; and various guides.

77 Gordon Dawes, 'A note on Guillaume Terrien and his work', *Jersey & Guernsey Law Review*, Feb 2007 https://www.jerseylaw.je/publications/jglr/Pages/JLR0702_Dawes.aspx [accessed 6 Mar 2017].

Advocates training: Duncan, *The History of Guernsey*, p 469.

A court unrivalled: *Guide to the Island of Guernsey*, 1826, pp 130-31.

London observer: anonymous review of Duncan's *The History of Guernsey*, in *Metropolitan Magazine*, vol 32, Sep-Dec 1841, p 49 https://books.google.com.au/books?id=TMARAAAAYAAJ [accessed 11 Jan 2016].

78 'no law in Guernsey': Duncan, *The History of Guernsey*, p 471. The law and justice in neighbouring Jersey attracted comparable comments, including Abraham Jones de Cras, *The laws, customs, and privileges, and their administration in the Island of Jersey*, Longman & Co, London, 1839.

'no *habeas corpus*': Berry, *The history of the island of Guernsey*, p 221. On Berry, see Crossan, *Guernsey, 1814-1914*, p 202.

'uncomfortable position': *L'Independance*, 5 Nov 1825.

Seven related jurats: Records of the Cour Royale, 19 Aug 1825.

On determination to defend existing political and legal structures, including the role of language in maintaining distinctiveness, see Crossan, *Guernsey, 1814-1914*, pp 237-38.

79 Hippisley case: *Star*, 22 Nov 1825. On Hippisley see: Elizabeth College Register, 1824-1873: With a Record of Some Earlier Students, https://archive.org/details/elizabethcolleg00guergoog; and his *A Narrative of the Expedition to the Rivers Orinoco and Apuré, in South America: Which Sailed from England in November 1817, and Joined the Patriotic Forces in Venezuela and Caráccas*, J. Murray, London, 1819. Hippisley appears as a colonel in his book, but is designated major in *Gazette*, 27 Aug 1825.

Murder: *Star*, 22 Nov 1825.

Timber theft: *Star*, 8 Nov 1825.

Cruelty to horses: *Gazette*, Aug 1825.

Insulting an officer: *Star*, 27 Sep 1825.

80 Mme Ollivier's cats: *L'Independance*, 28 May 1825; *Gazette*, 9 Aug, 20 Aug, 3 Sep 1825; *Star*, 9 Aug 1825.

Jean de Jersey's calumny: *Gazette*, 20 Aug 1825.

Respect or anarchy: *Star*, 6 Dec 1825.

Before the Cour Royale

85 I have reconstructed these speeches from the *Southampton Herald*, 7 Nov 1825, *Star*, 1 Nov 1825 (in English), and *L'Independance*, 5 Nov 1825 (in French). The account in *Gazette de Guernesey*, 5 Nov, appears to be a verbatim translation from English to French from the *Star*, even though the speeches of the court officials would have been delivered in French. For consistency, I have used the first person throughout.

Journal

93 The case involving Mary Ann Jones was heard by the Royal Court on 8 Oct 1825 and reported in the *Gazette de Guernesey*, 15 Oct. An earlier, but obscure, reference in the *Gazette* mentions Jean de Jersey's altercation with a Jurat. Jones's encounters with the Hospital can also be traced, confusingly, through *L'Hôpital Livre des Deliberations* 1822-1829, 6 Dec 1824; 7 Feb, 6 Apr, 6 Jun 1825, DC/HX 135-02, Island Archives, St Peter Port.

A letter from Mme Horne to M. de Campourcy

98 *Star*, 20 Dec 1825.

Journal

102 'great fat cobbler': Cecilia's expression, reported in the *Morning Post*, 13 Dec 1825.

A letter from Mr de Jersey to Mme Horne

105 *Star*, 20 Dec 1825.

Journal

106 Events of 18 Nov 1825 based chiefly on: *Star*, 22 Nov, 6 Dec, *Southampton Herald*, 12 Dec, *Morning Post*, 13 Dec.

A scene

110 Cecilia's oral testimony on 3 Dec has been assembled from varying, and sometimes

contradictory, reports in *Star*, 6 Dec, *Gazette de Guernesey*, 10 Dec, *L'Independance*, 10 Dec, and *Southampton Herald*, 12 Dec. Reports in the London press followed these sources. The *interrogatoires* are chiefly from *Gazette de Guernesey*, 10 Dec. For consistency, I have removed abbreviations and changed as necessary to the first person.

Journal

114 Events in Mme Stewart's parlour based chiefly on Brock's evidence in *Gazette de Guernesey*, 10 Dec, and Cecilia's testimony in *Star*, 6 Dec, *Gazette*, 10 Dec, and *Southampton Herald*, 12 Dec.

On evidence

117 De Jersey, Brock and de Campourcy on trial: Royal Court report, 22 Nov, 3 Dec 1825; *Star*, 29 Nov, 6, 17, 20 Dec; *L'Independance*, 3, 10 Dec; *Gazette de Guernesey*, 10 Dec; *Southampton Herald*, 12 Dec.
Unsigned article: *Star*, 22 Nov 1825.

118 Letter, 25 Nov 1825, setting things straight: *Gazette de Guernesey*, 26 Nov.
Au Public: *Gazette de Guernesey*, 3 Dec 1825.

120 French stuff : *Southampton Herald*, 12 Dec 1825, reproduced in London newspapers.
Religion in Guernsey: Duncan, *The History of Guernsey*, pp 356-69; *The Strangers' Guide to Guernsey; containing its situation, extent and population*, Guernsey, J E Collins, 1834, p 77; Crossan, *Guernsey, 1814-1914*, pp 191-95, 198-99; extract from Samuel Lewis, *Topographical Dictionary of England &c*, 1831, reproduced by Priaulx Library http://www.priaulxlibrary.co.uk/articles/article/st-peter-port-1831 [accessed 22 Feb 2017]. On anti-Catholicism, see memoir of the Rev Thomas Brock in John Jacob, *Annals of some of the British Norman Isles constituting the Bailiwick of Guernsey*, Part II, printed by J Smith, Paris, nd, pp 209-16.

121 A plain cross: *Southampton Herald*, 17 Dec 1825.
Cecilia's letter: *L'Independance*, 10 Dec 1825.

122 Most persuasive conclusion: William L Pressly, *The French Revolution as blasphemy: Johan Zoffany's paintings of the massacre at Paris, August 10, 1792*, University of California Press, Berkeley, 1999, p 133, p 15.

On history and fiction

125 The relationship between history and fiction is a perennial topic of discussion, revived each time a novelist or historian is judged to trespass too far into one or the other's territory: notable examples include Simon Schama's *Dead certainties: unwarranted speculations* (first published 1991), Kate Grenville's *The secret river* (first published 2005) and Julian Barnes's *The noise of time* (2016). I have drawn specific inspiration from Ann Curthoys and John Docker, *Is history fiction?* UNSW

Press, Sydney, 2006; Iain McCalman, 'Flirting with fiction', in Stuart Macintyre (ed), *The historian's conscience: Australian historians on the ethics of history*, MUP, Melbourne, 2004; Jill Lepore, 'Just the facts, Ma'am: Fake memoirs, factual fictions, and the history of history', *New Yorker*, 24 Mar 2008; Christine M. de Matos, "Fictorians: historians who 'lie' about the past, and like it", *TEXT: Journal of writing and writing programs*, vol 28, Apr 2015; Drusilla Modjeska, 'The informed imagination', *Meanjin*, vol 74, no 2, 2015; and Tom Griffiths, *The art of time travel: historians and their craft*, Black Inc, Carlton (Vic), 2016, esp chs 1 and 12.

129 'an interesting girl': *Morning Post*, 13 Dec 1825.

Denouements

131 Plaintive notice: *Gazette*, 18 Feb 1826.

'On Slander': *Gazette*, 14 Jan 1826.

132 Drury, Lang and Horne v Mauger: *Star*, 21 Feb 1826; *Gazette*, 25 Feb; *L'Independance*, 25 Feb.

Mauger's apology: *Gazette*, 1 Apr 1826.

133 Drury, Lang and Horne v de Jersey: *Star*, 14 Mar 1826; *Gazette*, 18 Mar; *L'Independance*, 18 Mar.

Thomas Horne (1800-70): entry by Mary Nicholls, *Australian Dictionary of Biography* http://adb.anu.edu.au/biography/horne-thomas-3798/text6013, published first in hardcopy 1972 [accessed 26 Feb 2017].

Will of Rev Thomas Horne (1772 -1847), 25 Jun 1844: http://www.genealogy.com/ftm/s/m/i/Heather-Smith-Manawatu/GENE4-0006.html [accessed 3 Jan 2015].

Eleanor Butler and Sarah Ponsonby: Elizabeth Mavor, *The ladies of Llangollen: a study in romantic friendship*, Penguin, London, 2001 (first published 1971).

Thanks

To those who read and commented on drafts at various times: Lali Foster, Michael McKernan, Mary Varghese and Audrey Young, all great encouragers; to my publisher in the United Kingdom, Stephen Foote, who edited the book with the expert knowledge of a local; and especially to Alan Atkinson, who brought to his reading an unsurpassed ear for language and eye for larger meanings.

To Simon Ross, Senior Deputy Greffier, who showed me around the Royal Court House at St Peter Port, including the Courtroom where Cecilia pleaded the natural rights of a mother in 1825; to staff at the Priaulx Library, where I spent many hours poring over original newspapers; to Jim Davidson, Kate Retford, Clare Rose, Carolyn Steedman and Penelope Treadwell, and colleagues at seminars at the Australian National University, for specific advice or pointers; and to Dale Horne, for information about the Horne family tree.

For help with translations from the French, to Anna Varghese and Gabrielle Hyslop.

Towards the end, to Adrian Young, without whose skills as a designer Cecilia's story might still be waiting to be told.

And above all, to Valsa.

Stephen Foster is an Australian historian who has spent much of his career at the borders of academic and public history. His books include *A Private Empire*, which was short-listed for the Ernest Scott Prize for History and the Victorian Premier's Literary Awards, and (as co-author) *The Making of the Australian National University*, which has been described as 'a model university history'. He and his wife have three adult children and two grandchildren.